WALKING THE ROYAL TRAIL

KUNGSLEDEN

WALKING THE ROYAL TRAIL
From Abisko to Hemavan

Claes Grundsten

Translated by Karin Cox

Carreg

First published in Great Britain in 2009 by
Carreg Limited
18 Parsons Croft
Hildersley
Ross-on-Wye
Herefordshire   HR9 5BN

ISBN 978 0 9538631 9 8

First published in Sweden in 2008 by Prisma, Stockholm.

The cover photograph shows a walker on the way to the
Kebnekaise Fellstation, with Duolbagorni in the background.

Printed and bound in the UK by 4word Ltd, Bristol.

Preface to English Edition

Kungsleden, the 400km walking route through Arctic Sweden, is one of the finest long-distance footpaths in Europe. It is also one of the best adventures, involving not only walking, but boat crossings, as well as the chance to climb Kebnekaise, Sweden's highest peak, and the possibility of spotting some of Europe's most elusive animals and birds. Until now there has not been an English-language guidebook to the magnificent route. The Swedish original of this guide was written and photographed by Claes Grundsten and includes not only an excellent guide to the route, but a collection of fine day-walks which the walker can enjoy, and details of the ascent of Kebnekaise. Claes has been a fell walker and mountaineer since childhood and is today one of Sweden's best-known nature photographers. After studying biology and physical geography at university he worked on vegetation-mapping in the Swedish mountains before working for the Swedish Environmental Protection Agency where we was responsible for planning and maintaining the country's mountain National Parks. Since 1993 he has been an acclaimed freelancer. He won Nature Photographer of the Year in Sweden in 1996, and the WWF Pandaprize in 2000. He has produced 25 books, several of which have been translated into English, including *Our Magnificent Wilderness*, *Trek!* and *Sarek and Kebnekaise where the light is ever-changing*. His website can be found at www.fotograf-grundsten.se.

The publishers are grateful to Karin Cox for her dedicated translation from the Swedish original. Karin Cox (née Düring) was born in Göteborg, and already in her schooldays she dreamt of walking the King's Way. She studied English, Phonetics and Theology at Uppsala University, and later trained in Edinburgh as a speech and language therapist. For several years she lived in the Lake District and enjoyed fell-walking there. She now lives in Cheltenham with her husband John, near to their three daughters and two grandchildren. She is glad to have walked the King's Way vicariously while translating this book, and hopes to get there one day before 'hanging up her boots'.

Please note that although 'Kungsleden' translates as King's Way, the now official name of the route in Sweden is The Royal Trail.

Abisko
National Park
Abisko
2
1
3
4
5a
Kebnekaise
5b   5c
6
Nikkaluokta
7
Kiruna
8
Stora Sjöfallets
National Park
Padjelanta
National Park
9
Saltoluokta
Sarek
National Park
10
Malmberget/Galliva
11
12
Kvikkjokk
13
14
15
16
17
Jäkkvik
Pieljekaise
National Park
19
18
21
20
22
25   23
Ammarnäs
24
26
28
27
Hemavan
Jokkmokk
Arvidsjaur

CONTENTS

INTRODUCTION

A Brief History of the Royal Trail

The Royal Trail is an old and well-known Swedish institution, which would lead people to believe it is also well planned and purposefully laid out. Many would also believe that there is a specially formed organisation caring for the route, its huts and bridges, boats and signs. But the reality is that the route through the Lapland fells has, to a large extent, been realised without any specific planning and that there is a complete lack of co-ordination regarding the route's upkeep.

From the beginning, the Trail was a child of the Svenska Turistföreningen (STF), a charitable organisation. With modest means, STF laid the foundation for the path we see today just over a hundred years ago as a result of a suggestion by the STF Committee secretary, Louis Améen. He had been inspired by the Russian Tsar who had built a railway between St. Petersburg and Moscow, creating a straight line on the map. The STF Committee drew a similar line from Abisko to Kvikkjokk, and decided that a *Kungsleden* (literally King's Way, though today the STF refer to the path as the Royal Trail) should follow that route, envisaging a cairned route with overnight huts, managed ford crossings and using rowing boats to cross lakes where required.

Thanks to the new railway to Narvik, access to Torneträsk had improved considerably, and by 1900 three suitable sites for huts between Torneträsk and Stora Sjöfallet had been identified, though it took another 40 years before any of them had been constructed as STF had limited financial resources and, at the time, there was no national body in charge of fell routes. The first huts to be built were at Abiskojaure and Kebnekaise, both opened in 1907. A year later some tourist *kåtor* (a *kåta* is a cone-shaped hut: *kåtor* is the plural of *kåta*) were erected south of Alesjaure, below Tjäktjapasset, at Guobirjohka (west of Kebnekaise) and on the shores of Teusajaure, and these remained in place for many years. STF also provided six rowing boats at the lakes that have to be crossed between Abisko and Vakkotavare. Hjalmar

Lundbohm, the founder of the Kiruna iron-ore mine, donated the Abisko hut, but that soon became too small and was extended in 1911. At Kaitumjaure and Vakkotavare *kåtor* were put up a few years later. Yet despite all this effort, the Royal Trail remained just a concept. In a guidebook of walks around Abisko, which STF published in 1914, there is no mention of the Trail as a name in itself, and when the fell pioneer and sketcher Th. S. Gudjohnsen produced his unique and hand-drawn guidebook of Kebnekaise in 1920, he described the section southwards from Abisko to Kebnekaise under the title *Alesvaggeleden*. Not until 1925 did STF get a firmer hold on tourism on the fells and produce a plan for expansion over the following ten years. Between 1926 and 1927, the path from Abisko to Vakkotavare was cairned with the help of Boy Scouts. Then, when the tourist station at Kvikkjokk was completed a year later, STF started to use the name *Kungsleden* for the first time, although there was never any official inauguration. After a few more years, *prisma* huts (a type of small hut) were built at Sälka, Singivagge and Alesjaure. All the huts were situated in the wilderness, difficult work given that there was no road access and limited financial resources. But interest in walking the route was increased, new *kåtor* sprang up, and the route was quietly extended southwards. In STF's 1941 yearbook, Nils Fröling, a legendary fell manager, wrote that the Royal Trail linked Abisko and Jäkkvik.

Next, in the early 1950s, STF drew up new guidelines for establishing fell routes and talked about the Trail being extended as far south as Ammarnäs. In 1955 Svante Lundgren, the famous photographer, wrote in a book titled *Kungsleden*, which stated that the route ended at Ammarnäs. But at the same time a number of fell walkers were maintaining that the Trail extended much further, comprising all the paths through the Swedish fells that STF had cairned, from Treriksröset ('the cairn of the three Kingdoms', where Finland, Norway and Sweden meet) to Grövelsjön. Clearly there was no agreement about the definition of the Trail.

During the 1960s and 1970s new huts were constructed on the sites of many of the old huts, and in 1975 *Kungsleden* was officially extended from Ammarnäs to Hemavan, an extension that coincided with the establishment of the Vindelsfjällen Nature Reserve. A significant change then took place in 1977, when the national route system in the fells was created, the Trail being incorporated into it. The Swedish Environmental Protection Agency was given the responsibility for this route system, laying the foundation for a maintenance system for the Trail, which is still in place. Many organisations and agencies are involved in this. STF owns most of the huts and has a field organisation for looking after them. STF also produces a great deal of information about the Trail. The Department for the Protection of the Natural Environment has overall responsibility for all fell routes and receives an annual amount from the public treasury to finance the work. Maintenance includes, among other things, waymarking the Trail, putting up signposts in strategic places, laying out *spänger* (the extended footbridges or boardwalks), and the building of bridges and shelters. All practical work is carried out by the County Councils of Norrbotten and Västerbotten, each of which has its own field organisation. The boat crossings along the Trail are provided by the local population, or in some cases by the warden of a tourist hut: these people are crucial if the route is to function for walkers. The reindeer-farming communities and the committees for safety on the fells are also involved in the care of the route, as are other agencies including the central tourist organisations, which are financed by the state. The task of the tourist organisations is to provide information about the Royal Trail to other countries so that the route can become better known internationally. As a consequence, the number of foreign walkers is steadily increasing.

This wide distribution of responsibility for the Trail has some detrimental consequences. Overall planning is still lacking, which means, for instance, that the section between Kvikkjokk and Jäkkvik is in need of improvement: the path needs to be cleared in places, the signposting needs improving, and a wish list would also include the building of several new huts to make it possible to walk the whole of *Kungsleden* without having to carry a tent. I also think that there should be a special organisation co-ordinating the maintenance and the development of the Trail in its entirety. A walking route with this long history and future potential, and which takes the walker through the country's most beautiful landscapes, deserves loving and effective supervision: *Kungsleden* represents Swedish heritage and, if managed and promoted in a professional way, can promote nothing but goodwill towards Sweden.

Why walk the Royal Trail?

'Walking is man's best medicine', wrote the father of medicine, Hippocrates, around 2500 years ago, and one can guess that he would have had the same opinion today, in spite of all the advanced medicines available. When we use our legs, muscles are strengthened, the brain is purified and our mental stamina is built up. In short, one becomes fitter, and walking is, after all, man's primeval method of locomotion in all kinds of terrain. If we walk far and long, a stroll becomes a hike.

One could also agree with Henry David Thoreau that 'to walk is to make a long journey in a short distance'. His philosophy appeals to me. During a hike the speed is approximately 3km/hr, a very humane speed, allowing time to look around. Many wise words have been formulated over the centuries about the blessing of walking. In modern parlance one could also say that walking is a form of preventive healthcare. You can start near your home and, gradually you will, I hope, have the urge to find new pastures. That is when you have become a walker in heart and soul. And then the Royal Trail is a path to dream about.

Hikes in the Swedish fells are my highlights as a walker. I can even say that they are the happiest moments in my life. But fell walking is not something I do only to keep fit. Health is rather a consequence of the hikes. Above all I want to get out into a magnificent landscape and feel its pulse, and to get to know myself and my fellow walkers at a deeper level. We come close to each other on the fells. During the walk, life is simple, following the rhythms of day and night, and the weather. Senses are awakened, and the variations in the landscape become a main theme in the experience, the scenery keeping our attention alive. The Swedish mountains have a soft character with their sweeping contours, yet I do not know any other landscape that can change so abruptly from sensuous shape to brutal appearance, rounded hills transforming into threatening precipices. For long distances we follow a valley below soothing mountains or walk across an endless plain, but at times genuine alps appear, with glaciers and steep mountainsides. *Kungsleden* provides us with this whole spectrum.

The Trail also provides opportunities for exciting encounters with flora and fauna. Some years there is an abundance of small rodents in the mountains, and the birdlife becomes richer than normal. And memorable if the walker comes, quite unexpectedly, into the territory of a Long-tailed Skua and has defend to him or her self against the bird's bombing raids. Or to hear the solitary call of a Rough-legged Buzzard under a precipice. And they are merely two examples. And how fascinating to discover a scrub heath abundant with beautiful alpine flowers. Or the clicking trot of the reindeer across a mountain plateau – always a welcome sound.

In spite of all this, in spite of the fact that the advantages for health are evident and that being near nature is a great experience, I wish to say that for me the greatest reward from mountain walks is at another and deeper level: it is freedom. Think of the various kinds of freedom offered by a mountain: freedom from everyday duties, the noise of the city, bosses and decision makers who rule it over you, traffic and stress, news and media. The peace and quiet of mountain scenery is an immeasurable asset. Here we have the chance to do what we wish with our days. We can think and meditate, study nature or just be together, stress-free. We are our own masters, and the scenery is like the incarnation of the concept of freedom, with its wide plains, long valleys and challenging summits.

Many people who have not tried mountain walking think that it is difficult and demands considerable knowledge and extreme fitness. But that is not the case. We can plan the walks according to our own abilities, and here I give some general advice and tips to those who wish to walk the Royal Trail.

Huts

The most popular parts of the King's Way have overnight huts at each end of a daily walk section that are maintained by Svenska Turistföreningen. There are usually bunk beds and blankets in multi-occupied rooms. This means there is no need to carry a sleeping bag (important when weight is a factor), though I do recommend that you take a sheet sleeping bag. The standard in the huts is basic: there is no electricity, though they do have woodburners and latrines. Some also have a sauna. Walkers are expected to chop wood, fetch water and clean up after themselves. There is often a drying room. Water is fetched in buckets from streams outside the hut. There is no catering – walking the Trail is on a self-catering basis. There is a gas stove in every hut on which you can prepare your own food, the stove being shared with other walkers. Every hut has a warden who looks after the hut during the high season, and also collects fees. The charge in 2008 was 315 SEK per night for non-members and 215 SEK for members of STF. You cannot book a bed in advance, but there is always space for everyone – in emergency it will be on the floor. During low season there is always safe storage available. In several of the huts there is a small shop where you can replenish your provisions during high season. Another positive factor with the huts is the companionship: you meet other walkers in a relaxed atmosphere, and you can share your experiences after the day's adventures. The huts also provide a place of safety in bad weather. There are also many small shelters along the way, which offer protection when it is raining.

One great advantage of the huts is that you can keep the weight of your load down. You do not need to bring a cooking stove, sleeping bag, sleeping mat or tent. But this applies only to those stretches of the Trail that have huts at the ends of each daily section. These are Abisko–Vakkotavare (and Nikkaluokta), Saltoluokta–Kvikkjokk and Ammarnäs

–Hemavan. On the remaining two stretches (Kvikkjokk–Jäkkvik and Jäkkvik–Ammarnäs) a tent is essential for overnight stays. Of course you can carry a tent anywhere along the Trail. I personally prefer camping, as it offers greater freedom: you can spend the night wherever you wish and the day's journey can be planned according to your individual wishes. I also value another aspect of camping: you spend all your time in the open and experience the changes in the weather. In a hut you shut out nature. But your backpack will undoubtedly be heavier, it is not as comfortable to sleep on the ground as in a bed, and cooking is more complicated, especially if it rains. One alternative is to camp by the huts and to use the facilities there. For this there is a charge of 60 SEK, or 40 SEK for members of STF.

The best sections

Which section of The King's Way is the best to walk? This question has no obvious answer, as the character of the route is ever changing. As will be clear from my guide text, we can divide the route into five naturally cohesive stretches. Every section corresponds to a suitable fell walk of about a week or more, but the sections have different characters and make different demands. The most popular and best known stretch is the one between Abisko and Nikkaluokta. Here you will find many walkers, and at the end of every day there is an overnight hut. This is the classic section of the Trail, and it is highly recommended for those new to the Swedish fells. Thanks to the huts, and the fact that there are usually many walkers around, the route feels especially safe, even in adverse weather conditions. I have walked this section many times and get just as deeply affected by the beauty and the atmosphere of the landscape every time. If you walk to Nikkaluokta, there is also the possibility of climbing Kebnekaise (Sweden's highest mountain: the peak's name means 'cauldron'), a truly memorable trip.

The decision to head for Nikkaluokta means leaving the Trail rather than continuing along it to Vakkotavare. The latter is somewhat less frequented by walkers, many being intent on climbing Kebnekaise, but in terms of natural beauty the route to Vakkotavare is comparable. The huts at Kaitumjaure and Teusajaure are particularly beautifully, being situated by some of the most fjord-like lakes in the fell region. Alternatively, one can of course walk from Nikkaluokta to Vakkotavare, or in the opposite direction, and I maintain that this is as rewarding a walk as the one from Abisko.

Kungsleden between Saltoluokta and Kvikkjokk is also a classic walk, though the landscape is not as dramatic, apart from Aktse and the gateway to Sarek. One could probably say that the landscape around Aktse stands in a class by itself, both along the Trail and in Sweden as a whole. Of course if you get here, you will have to climb Skierffe from where there is a unique view of the fells towards the Rapa delta. For the person with limited time for walking, I recommend this section of the Trail. It can be walked over four days, but a couple of the day sections are unusually long and tiring.

South of Kvikkjokk the Trail becomes desolate and very different, the day walks being long and not as naturally defined. Indeed, this is true for the whole route south as far as Ammarnäs. If you choose to walk these sections, you will have to carry a tent, and you have to expect a different kind of fell landscape to that in the north, with less dramatic landscapes, but with overwhelming, boundless views and long stretches of walking in fell forest. I believe that this part of the Trail is for the seasoned fell walker, someone wishing to explore deserted areas and looking to experience more of the variety Lapland has to offer. In my opinion these sections of the Trail are underestimated.

Between Ammarnäs and Hemavan the route becomes easy to walk again, thanks to well-situated huts. I am personally very fond of this section, which offers a variety of scenery, the walking being more varied than anywhere else along the route.

The best time

Walking in the fells is possible between July and September, the peak season being end July/early August. That said, there is an advantage in

15

walking during June as the birdlife is abundant, the mosquitoes are still few in number, there is plenty of space in the huts, and it is light around the clock. The disadvantage is that streams and rivers can overflow, and that there may still be plenty of snow at high altitudes. During July the flowers are stunningly beautiful and it can be really warm. But the mosquitoes and biting midges are swarming and can, at times, be a real plague. The huts can also be rather crowded. During August the evenings begin to be dark, and a torch is needed. But the rivers are usually at a low level and by the end of the month the mosquitoes are markedly reduced in numbers. September is the month I regard as the best time for fell expeditions. The plague of mosquitoes has gone, the air is clear and crisp, and the colours are brilliant in the forest and on the heath. If the summits are powdered with new-fallen snow, the views are at their best, and at that time there is also a greater chance of seeing big game – Bear, Wolverine and Elk. The downside is that bird-life is scant.

Risks

Long distance walks are an adventure. They bring challenges and hardships, but everyone experiences the demands in different ways. I would prefer to call *Kungsleden* a moderately strenuous adventure. It is relatively risk-free to walk, and it is a trek that can suit most people with normal fitness, though difficult for those with serious physical handicaps. In the main the route is easy to follow, making map work and compass straightforward. On the whole it is not necessary to negotiate any sizeable rivers by wading, the larger rivers now having been bridged.

But there are three things I do need to mention, each of which can make walking the Trail troublesome: mosquitoes and midges, blisters and bad weather. How you cope with the insects is a very personal matter. There is a lot of psychology involved – it really is, in part at least, a question of attitude. Anti-midge preparations are often effective, but if you are exceptionally sensitive, I also recommend that you bring a mosquito hat with a net to cover the face. These are effective but a bit cumbersome if you wish to eat in the open. Blisters are best prevented by wearing well broken-in boots. It is also important to wash the feet regularly, to change into clean socks often, to air the feet when having a rest, and to cut one's toenails. Bad weather is best coped with by carrying good waterproof wear. Remember that you can actually encounter snowstorms even in summertime. The greatest risk with storms is that you may become exhausted, particularly if walking into a strong headwind. Therefore make sure you bring high carbohydrate food or glucose, which gives instant energy.

Equipment for hut tours

First a well tested piece of advice, which is always relevant: only take as much as you really need during the walk, and always try to make your equipment as light as possible. During a hut tour the rucksack should not weigh more than a maximum of 15kg, preferably less. Buy a well-fitting rucksack of good quality and with a detachable rainproof cover. There are many models available to buy. It should hold at least 50 litres. In the rucksack you must carry a light sleeping bag or a sheet sleeping bag. A small seatpad to put on the ground when having a rest is useful, as it weighs so little. A light plastic water bottle, matches, whistle, sunglasses and knife are necessary equipment. A thermos flask for hot drinks is needed for the lunchbreaks, and you can then make do without a camping stove. A beaker needs to be kept handy. There are folding ones that can be carried in a trouser pocket. Spare clothing is best carried in a waterproof bag. The following items are required: spare socks and spare pants, gloves, scarf, warm hat and warm sweater or a padded gilet or light padded jacket. Rainwear, jacket and trousers, is a necessity, and it needs to be both waterproof and breathable. The most frequently seen brand is Goretex, but there are also other, similar fabrics. It is also a good idea to have an outer pair of gloves or mittens in the same material as if it rains and, at the same time, there is a strong wind, your hands can easily get cold. The jacket must have a hood so it can also be used as a windproof in strong winds, even if it is not raining. Waterproof trousers with zips along the legs have the advantage of allowing them to be put on without taking the boots off.

While walking, it is preferable to wear an airy shirt and trekking trousers with leg pockets. I prefer dividable trousers which can be converted into shorts, and in the leg pockets I keep a whistle (in case you need to attract attention), a small compass, a clasp knife and a mini pair of binoculars. I wear a vest if the weather is cool; otherwise it is kept in the spare clothes bag. Sometimes I take a very light windproof shirt. Toiletries like soap, a small towel, a short toothbrush and a small tube of toothpaste are of course essentials. Also remember to bring toilet paper in a waterproof bag. A map is mandatory, but think twice about taking a mobile phone. In the fells the signal is virtually non-existent, except on the high peaks. At the starting points it is usually OK, but only if your phone company has a deal with Telia, the Swedish telecommunication company.

Footwear is always a matter for discussion between walkers. Let me first say that a pair of light manmade slippers is a useful extra for life in the huts, and I think these should be carried, even if they add a few hundred grams to the weight. Out on the paths you must wear well-broken-in footwear. Some walkers prefer Wellington boots, but while these are useful on boggy ground, there is little of that on the Trail. I therefore rather recommend boots, but the question is whether they should be high- or low-legged. An advantage of high bootlegs is the protection they provide when wading, and perhaps also the ankle support. But these days I prefer the low-legged boots, which are naturally lighter and more flexible. To save on the weight of footwear is important, as there is an opinion that says that the weight you load on your feet requires much more energy than carrying the same weight in the rucksack. Lightweight boots also make the walking easier. With the boots I use a pair of low gaiters, which I put on if the ground is full of clay, or at small easy wading places. The boots should have Goretex linings, which make them waterproof, without the feet becoming sweaty.

Trekking poles are useful, and I recommend them. I bring a pair, but prefer to walk with just one, keeping the second in reserve in case I twist my ankle or am hit by other problems that make it difficult to walk. A small first aid box with plaster, bandages, creams and medication you can share with your walking companion is also useful. And the same is true of a bag of repair items, e.g. steel wire, sewing aids, and perhaps boot wax.

Starting points on the Royal Trail

Kungsleden is naturally divided into five sections, which link the few roads that penetrate westwards into the fells. However, the Trail often passes villages that can be reached by public transport (which means buses apart from the train at Abisko). Sections of the Trail often use these villages as starting-points.

Abisko (Altitude 385m)

Abisko means 'the forest near the sea'. The fell station here was established in 1902, the current building having been constructed in 1952 after the old one was destroyed by fire. In order to be more fire resistant, the new building is a brick construction. But despite it being more functional than beautiful, the station has a deeply ingrained charm. In 1983 the road along Torneträsk was opened and, as a consequence, the character of Abisko changed from being rather like a health resort to becoming a modern tourist resort. In the 1980s the fell station was complemented by a cabin village and an annex for walkers. At the same time the Swedish Environmental Protection Board built a 'Nature Room' with a permanent exhibition of the alpine world.

The principal fell station building is situated on a small hill above the Abiskojåkka canyon. The view is stunning across Torneträsk, and the immediate surroundings are protected in the Abisko National Park. In front of the main entrance is a pleasant 'fell garden', where many alpine plants can be studied. The Abisko station is one of the best starting points for walks on the Swedish fells: apart from being a wonderfully beautiful area, there are many interesting places within easy distance. Abisko also has the advantage of a favourable climate, its rain shadow position providing one of the sunniest climes in Sweden. The fell station has 300 beds, a restaurant and a shop selling food, maps, guides, etc.

Nikkaluokta (470m)

The village of Nikkaluokta is said to have been named after a fisherman named Nikolaus, his name regularly shortened to Nikku, who had a hut nearby. However, another story maintains the village was named after Nils Sarri who, in 1910, settled here with his wife Maria. They had 14 children, and Nils worked as a fell guide for STF, several of his children doing the same. Over the years, many tourists have been taken up Kebnekaise by guides from the Sarri family, and the family still runs the tourist trade in the area. Petter Haugli, another STF worker, made his home in Nikkaluokta at the same time as Sarri. In total there were five families in the village when it began, the others having earlier been nomadic Sámi who spent their summers west of Narvik, and gradually the landscape around Nikkaluokta was altered by their haymaking and by their grazing animals, both cows and goats. On a high gravel ridge above the village a beautiful little chapel was built in 1942, a highly visible landmark. After many years of not being served by a permanent road, a road to the village was finally opened in 1971. The journey along the road is through a wonderful landscape that heightens the desire to get out on the fells. The village itself merely accentuates this desire. Situated at the western end of Paittasjärvi, a large lake set where two large fell valleys, Láddjurvággi and Visttasvággi, meet, Nikkaluokta is where the Kebnekaise range of mountains begins, and the views, with a backdrop of high summits, are among the most magnificent in Sweden.

Nikkaluokta is now a modern tourist centre with a restaurant, cabins for hire, a service building with showers and sauna, and an art gallery Skáidi, which usually has fine exhibitions.

Saltoluokta (390m)

Saltoluokta is often referred to as the pearl of the older fell stations in Lapland. It is situated in a place of great natural beauty, embedded in an area of Alpine Birch (*Betula czerepanovii*, a sub-species of White Birch *B. pubescens*) and surrounded by monumental mountain scenery in Sjöfallsdalen. The region offers rich contrasts between the Alpine Birch forest, Lake Langas, and the dark, high rock of the Lulep Kierkau fell, a landscape that provides a peaceful harmony, which is unusual, even for the fells, particularly when evening light gilds the scenery. The sun in the west can make the water glisten and shimmer against a backdrop of shadowy black mountain precipices. And when the sun breaks through clouds, there are occasionally wonderful light effects in Sjöfallsdalen.

The name Saltoluokta has a remarkable history. The place was originally called Kaltoluokta, which means 'the cove of the spring'. The cartographer who recorded the name wrote his 'K' carelessly, and it was interpreted as an 'S' when it was included on the map. The incorrect name Saltoluokta later became the name of the STF fell station, and it is now generally accepted even among the local Sámi.

In 1912 the first overnight hut was built here, the main timber building being completed in 1918. It comprises a beautiful dining room, communal room and guestrooms with no water. Altogether the site has almost 100 beds, divided between several buildings. For campers there is a service building with kitchen, sauna, showers and drying room.

Kvikkjokk (330m)

Kvikkjokk village is the oldest of the entrance points to the Lapland fells. It is in an idyllic location at the edge of a fertile delta built up by the Tarraätno and Kamajokk rivers, just where these merge and run into Lake Sakkat. The name Kvikkjokk is a 'Swedification' of the two Sámi words for 'rapid' and 'large brook'. The houses in the village are spread across the forest-covered slope above the water labyrinth of the delta, surrounded by pine trees and open fields. In the surrounding area, valley stands against mountain, pine forest against open fell, forest gloom against open water, barren land against pasture: here we meet the last outpost of civilisation before the wilderness. The 100km long road reaching out to the village also creates a feeling of an out-of-the-way corner in a way that few other places in the fells provide. The road, which starts at Jokkmokk, was completed in 1957. It follows the lake chain of Lilla Lule river westwards, running parallel to the towering precipices that border the lakes to the south. The road runs through wild forest country and then, as you approach Kvikkjokk, the scenery grows in grandeur. Just before the village, the road runs along the beautiful shores of Lake Sakkat, the majestic summit of Staika in Tarradalen in the west coming into view. The view signals the end of the road at the foot of the fells.

Kvikkjokk village has its origin in the second half of the 17th century, when the mines in Silpatjåkkå and Alkavare were operating, the ore being processed in a smelting-hut, which required access to firewood and waterpower. Where the rapid waters of Kamajåkkå run into Lake Sakkat, these natural resources were available, and in 1662 the first trial smelting took place at the Kvikkjokk silver works. After 40 years of activity, the smelting-house was closed, as the ore veins had been exhausted. During the period of mine activity the village was much larger, and at certain times village councils were held, the villagers gathering a large stone by a now-felled pine tree (the stone is 3km north of the village and is marked on the local map). After the closure of the silver works the village survived thanks to the clergy, the buildings of the smelting works being placed in the care of the vicar, the Lapland mission among the Sámi continuing with Kvikkjokk as a centre. A simple church was built in the 1760s, but the population remained small until the middle of the next century when settlers from both inland and the coast arrived, bringing new life to the village. A new church was built during the years 1906–07 at which time the number of villagers was just over 40.

The villagers' interest in agriculture and cattle rearing faded after the 1939–45 War, the disappearance of the cattle ending haymaking on the delta. In 1956 the last sedge harvest took place, and in 1968 the last meadow harvest, the natural landscape around the delta then being re-established. On the flooded plains, willow and birch saplings had been cleared in order to ensure a better sedge harvest, while barley and rye had been cultivated in the central section of the delta from the 18th century onwards, with cattle grazing on the westernmost islets. With all this land-use discontinued nature recolonised the land.

After Carl von Linné's journey to Lapland in 1732 when he passed Kvikkjok, the village attracted more attention than most other villages in Lapland, so that when tourism began people began to find their way to the village. Then, in 1928 the STF fell station was built on a ridge by the constantly roaring rapids of Kamajåkkå. The station is one of the more pleasant starting points for a walk. It consists of two newly renovated buildings, and has a restaurant as well as self-catering facilities. There are also a shop and communal room. The station has 58 beds: there are also other overnight facilities in the village.

Jäkkvik (440m)

Jäkkvik is a small village on the shores of Hornavan, the deepest lake in Sweden. The Silver Road (National Road 95) passes through the village. It was at Jäkkvik that the revivalist preacher Lars Levi Laestadius was born in 1800, a stone memorial to his memory marking his birthplace on a promontory into the lake. The village has had a permanent population since 1840, the famous chapel built in 1777 at Lövmokk being moved to Jäkkvik in 1885, as by then the village had become the meeting-place for people living in the inner part of the Arjeplog mountain area. The chapel was originally situated north of the village by an inlet of Hornavan called Tjårvekallagiehtje: the small, beautiful building has become famous as a result of a painting by Johan Fredrik Höckert called *Worship in Lövmokk Chapel*. The painting, inspired by the work of Rembrandt, can be seen in the Swedish

National Museum in Stockholm. Today the village has about 30 permanent residents. Accommodation is offered, if there is room, in the Church Fell Centre, which has 60 beds.

Ammarnäs (402m)

Ammarnäs was established around 1820, close to the 'potato hill', a high mound of gravel formed during the Ice Age. On the mound's steep south side, potatoes (a particular, elongated variety known throughout Sweden as 'almond potatoes') have been cultivated for more than 100 years. Other visible results of the local people's laborious cultivation can be seen across the landscape, haymaking meadows and grazing pastures lightening the dark spruce forest that surrounds the village. The islets in the fertile delta in Gautsträsk lake are scattered with picturesque hay-barns, sometimes with the high water mark of the spring flood right up to the eaves. These beautifully-aged barns are still in use today, as are the magnificent slopes where cows graze the lush grass during the summer. The open fields and the settlements lie on the west side of Gautsträsk and climb up the slopes of Näsberget, one of the few summits visible above the forested mountain ridges around the village. On Näsberget, ski pistes look like broad streets through the forest.

Ammarnäs is a lively place, more vibrant than most other fell villages, a place where nature and culture merge, a place with a special atmosphere. About 300 people live here today, in one of the longest cul-de-sacs in the fell country, the road from Sorsele being almost 90km long. Within the village there is a choice of accommodation, in youth hostels, cabin villages and hotels. In the surrounding country there are opportunities for many excellent excursions, a trip to the top of Potato Hill offering a great view of the village.

Hemavan (356m)

As with Abisko, Hemavan has been affected by the busy road that passes through the village. The extensive ski resorts, cabin villages and, not least, the unique tower with its cupola at the visitor centre, underline the inevitable impression of a modern conurbation. Nevertheless the natural surroundings are magnificent, with Norra Storfjället rising 1000m above the village. To the west you can see Arfjället, often sprinkled white with snow right through the summer, and from the restaurant in the nature room cupola it is even possible to see the mountains of Norway. The surrounding area, in the Ume river valley from Tärnaby to the Norwegian border, including the Tängvatten and Joesjö valleys, mixes extensive birch forest with still-active farms.

The possibilities for accommodation are exceptionally good in Hemavan and the surrounding smaller villages, with several hotels and cabin villages. If you start or finish your walk along the Trail in Hemavan, a visit to the Fell Botanic Garden, on the slope behind the tower and cupola, is worthwhile: the garden is a unique creation, 'smuggled' into the natural birch forest, with 430 species of fell flora, grasses, trees and ferns. Of the plants about half are wild species, the rest being cultivated. All the plants are very well tended and arranged with clear plots and labels.

Reading the Route Descriptions

Which direction is the most natural for walking the Royal Trail, heading north or south? Approximately two-thirds of walkers head south, particularly along the most popular sections between Abisko, Kebnekaise and Vakkotavare, and this direction feels the most natural for me. When I walked the whole Trail in one continuous journey in 2007, my walk started in Abisko and ended in Hemavan. The question of direction of travel sounds academic, but it is very relevant when writing a guide, as views etc. are described as they appear along the path, and so a complete guide should include a description of both directions. But that would require the text to be twice as long. The text describes the Trail from Abisko to Hemavan, a distance of 420km, but I am sure that walkers who go in the opposite direction will still benefit from the information.

Is the Trail difficult to walk? That is a difficult question as there is considerable variation in the way individuals experience the physical effort involved. Whether a walk is considered easy or demanding depends a great deal on external conditions: whether the weather is good or bad is important; the weight of the rucsac is another central factor; and basic physical fitness is of course of the greatest importance. The way the day develops also plays a role. Scenery affects our psyche, a beautiful view making the walking easier than no view at all. Added to this is the character of the path and the terrain. The route can be hilly, stony, boggy, long or short: conditions are constantly changing. All these factors make the objective grading of trekking routes complicated. But even so walkers all like to have an idea of what to expect before setting out. I have read guidebooks which, with their own tailor-made systems, list the characteristics of the paths. In my early books I used three grades of difficulty: easy, difficult and very difficult. In this guide I have changed the system to make it clearer. I have given every section of the Trail an overall category based on the effort involved as I experienced it. I use the following categories:

Easy: a section which is exceptionally short (less than 10km), or which has few climbs and a level and well-trodden path.

Normal: applies to sections of about 12–15km, without too much climbing, and with a path that is level and easily walked – that is to say average.

Strenuous: long sections, around 20km or more, and sections that have a difficult path because the ground is stony or boggy, or where there is wading. Also in this category come shorter sections with hard climbs and sections that require camping equipment.

Another factor influencing the experience of a section is that we walk at a varying pace. The estimated time I give applies only to the length of time one is actually walking. I have not taken into account how many or how long the breaks a walker might take will be, for this varies endlessly. The actual walking pace also varies a great deal from person to person. What is a normal walking pace is always a matter for discussion. In the Swedish fells we usually think in terms of 3–4km per hour on a well-trodden walking route, but how fast one manages to walk depends on all the physical factors I have mentioned earlier. Another thing to consider is that we get more tired towards the end of a day. There is also a rule of thumb that says we should usually add a half-hour for every 300m of ascent. On a descent the pace increases naturally, but only if the gradient is not too great: steeper descents involve a slower pace than level ground. The figures given in this book have been estimated with these norms in mind. On the day-excursions I have also taken into account that the rucsac will be lighter. The time estimated is given with a variation of about two hours: hopefully that variation will be enough to cater for differences from person to person.

Distance and altitude differences

Along the Trail the walker will find numerous signposts showing distances. These are usually accurate enough, and I have used them as far as possible, but sometimes they are dubious and even contradictory. I have come across instances where there is one figure at one end of a section, and another at the other end. As a rule I then choose the higher figure. The day excursions in pathless country I have measured on the map using a standard measuring wheel. The error with these is about ±10%. Height differences have been calculated from contour lines. In most cases a walk includes both ups and downs, these distributed along the section. Ups are marked with a +, and downs with a -.

The maps in the guide are reproduced from the Lantmäteriets Fjällkarta 1:100,000 maps, which have been scaled to approximately 1:200,000.

Place names

Kungsleden passes through three language areas: North Sámi (between Abisko and Teusadalen), Lule Sámi (between Teusadalen and Adolfström) and South Sámi (between Adolfström and Hemavan). These dialects differ approximately as much as the Nordic languages. From having been entirely oral languages, the dialects were each given their own written form at the end of the 1970s/beginning of the 1980s, each of them with its own rules for spelling. And these spellings have now been included in the official fell maps. The background is a UN resolution that says that countries with minority language inhabitants should have their spelling represented on general maps of their areas. The phonetic spellings of Sámi place names on the old maps have therefore been changed to very different spellings. For instance, Kebnekaise is spelt Giebmegáisi, even if the pronunciation is approximately the same. To us fell walkers this means we have to learn three different spellings for the natural features. The earlier word for 'lake' was 'jaure'. Today 'lake' appears in three forms: jávri (North Sámi), jaure (Lule Sámi) and jávrrie (South Sámi). The previous word 'tjåkkå' for 'fell summit' is now spelt čohkka (North Sámi), tjåhkkå (Lule Sámi) and tjåhke (South Sámi).

The changes have without doubt created many problems, not least because many walkers find it difficult to manage the pronunciation of the new names. It has also become more complicated to relate names to older literature.

To make some form of compromise, the Lantmäteriets (the Swedish Ordnance Survey) has chosen to include the older Sámi place names on the map, if these are well known. Kebnekaise therefore appears in both the old and the new spelling on the map. When I now look through my previous guide texts about the Royal Trail, I update the text with the new place names as they appear on the current maps, but where the new map has the old spelling alongside, I prefer to use that, simply because it is better known and is easier to pronounce.

Day excursions

The day excursions in the book are only suggestions on my part. Many more excursions are possible from each of the huts along the Trail. I have concentrated on summit climbs and places of botanical, ornithological and geological interest, and historical monuments.

Summit climbs

My experience is that summit climbs are the highlights of a fell walk in all respects, and I strongly recommend that you try if the weather allows. One advantage with the Swedish fells is that most high summits can be reached without any advanced climbing being required. All the suggestions for excursions included in this book (except for the east path on Kebnekaise) are therefore walking ascents not requiring high mountain equipment such as rope, ice axe and crampons.

Places of botanical interest

Alpine plants attract strong affections, particularly those that grow in harsh conditions. Many paths along the Trail, and several day excursions, pass through areas that have a richer flora than normal. This applies especially to the vegetation on lime-rich soil, where the rarest plants are to be found, and where the flora is generally the most varied. I have included a number of excursions to such areas.

Places of ornithological interest

Birdwatching in the fells is relatively easy, due to the open character of the landscape. Certain areas with varied vegetation, for example willow thickets and bogs, have an exceptionally rich birdlife. This also applies to areas of dense meadow birch forest, and to the deltas in lakes and rivers. Such places are to be found in suggested day excursions.

Places of geological interest

The fells provide many places of geological interest. It is enriching to try to 'read' the contours of the landscape and to ponder its history and formation. I have included a number of such destinations. They may emphasise the bedrock, for example where beautiful crystals, interesting minerals or rocks may be found. There are also interesting landscapes formed by inland ice and glaciers, for instance boulder ridges, moraines and deltas. Even scars from landslides and other geological processes can be worth seeing.

Historic monuments

Even those fells that appear wild and uninhabited are likely to have a human history going back over many years. In many places you can see traces of man, mainly from the Sámi culture, but also from other settlers. Some of the suggested day excursions take you to memorials of reindeer keepers, or to old mines and settlements.

Abisko ·

Distance: 109km. Height gain/loss

This is the best known and most frequented section of the Royal Trail. In these still roadless and uninhabited fell regions, a trail was blazed at the beginning of the 20th century: the beginning of today's Trail. Here you walk right through the high fells to the west of the conglomeration of steep summits of Kebnekaise. Steep mountainsides are in view wherever you look, and the landscape varies from birch forest to high plain to deep valleys. Many walkers make a detour from the Trail, walking eastwards past the Kebnekaise fell station to finish their trek in Nikkaluokta. Perhaps you will climb to the 'roof of Sweden', the south summit of Kebnekaise.

On leaving Abisko, there is just over 10km of easy walking through the lush alpine birch forest of the National Park, which shares it name with the village. The next day's walk to Alesjaure is the longest, leaving the protection of the forest behind to emerge onto open fell. The path takes you through a magnificent valley with large lakes and alpine mountains, the day's end point being a large and comfortable collection of huts. From Alesjaure the valley trek continues southwards: during the next two days you climb up to the highest point on the Trail, Tjäktjapasset, at 1150m. Here the landscape is extremely barren, often with permanent snow amid high summits. From the pass you descend into the Tjäktjavagge valley, a broad avenue among the Kebnekaise fells. The valley is 30km long, and the Trail follows it in its entirety, passing Sälka, a famous point from where you can see many of the highest peaks in Sweden, the South Summit of Kebnekaise included. At the Singi huts there is the possibility of taking a detour on to the path that passes Kebnekaise fell station to reach Nikkaluokta. Southwards from Singi the landscape changes character again, becoming 'friendly', as it was in the Abisko National Park. At Kaitum you reach birch forest again, but still with views to dramatic mountain scenery.

Further on you cross wide, high plateaux with extensive views. After the first plateau you come to Teusadalen, which is one of the most beautiful valleys along the Trail. Next day, the walk takes you across another plateau, the views being the most expansive so far, the distant summits of Sarek being visible. A steep and difficult descent to Vakkotavare completes this stretch of the Trail.

1. Abisko – Abiskojaure

Distance: 13km. Height gain/loss: +105m. Time: 4–5 hours. Easy.

This day walk runs entirely within Abisko National Park. You walk through the lush dwarf birch forest in a wide valley with views to the high mountains south of Abisko. At Abiskojaure you reach an untouched mountain world, the built-up areas along the E10 road feeling very distant. The path is wide and well-trodden, and along the stretch nearest to the Abisko fell station you are likely to meet walkers on day tours.

Kungsleden starts by the car park beside the 'Abisko Tourist' railway station. A gateway with a signpost can be found 50m west of the car park, in the direction of Abiskojåkka. From this gateway you walk into the forest, and after about 100m the path branches at the imposing rock canyon of Abiskojåkka. The ravine is narrower and smaller here than on the other side of the railway, north of the E10 road, the fast-running river more squeezed together by the rocks. From the fork in the path it used to be possible to cross the 'Red Bridge' towards Kårsavagge, but the bridge has now been demolished.

The Trail now runs parallel to Abiskojåkka, about 10m into the forest from the river, as you walk southwards, upstream along a wide, well-trodden path, accompanied by the roar from the 25m wide torrent. On the other side of Abiskojåkka, i.e. on the west side, the terrain rises steeply to the rounded summit of Slåttatjåkka, this prominent mountain behind the line of trees giving the feeling of walking in a deep valley. The Trail crosses a number of extended boardwalks across wet ground, but the forest is mainly fairly dry: it is a mossy birch forest with Crowberries (*Empetrum nigrum*) and bilberries (*Vaccinium myrtillus* – usually called blueberries, both in Sweden and elsewhere) in the undergrowth. In the bogs there is a great variety of orchids, e.g. Small White Orchid (*Leuchorchis albida*) and Fragrant Orchid (*Gymnadenia conopsea*). In the forest there are also a number of pits – old gunning emplacements from defences built during the 1939–45 War when it was feared that a German invasion might come along the *Malmbanan* railway, and Sweden would need to halt the advance at Abiskojåkka.

After a couple of kilometres you arrive at the 'marble quarry', a 10m high limestone cliff beside the river, which forms a bend here. Marble, or rather dolomite (limestone rich in magnesium), was quarried here in the early 1900s. Here the Trail is joined by a path from Njakajaure, which starts in the eastern part of Abisko and goes over open sub-alpine moors (sub-alpine fell being a band below the open fell line). If you choose that path to get to this point, you have the chance of good birdwatching: on the moors you may, for instance, see Whimbrel and Whinchat.

The Trail passes over the highest point of the quarry, where there is a shelter with toilets and a table with seats, a well-known rest spot. Close by is a meditation place on the Dag Hammarskjöld Way, a project launched by the Church of Sweden. The Way links Abisko to Singi, continuing to Nikkaluokta. Along the Way there are seven places for meditation, each with a stone carved with a quotation from Dag Hammarskjöld's book *Vägmärken* (Markings). (Publisher's Note: Dag Hammarskjöld (1905–1961), a Swedish diplomat, was the second

Secretary-general of the United Nations, serving from 1953 until 1961 when he died in an air crash. He was awarded the Nobel Peace Prize, posthumously. US President John F. Kennedy called Dag Hammarskjöld 'the greatest statesman of our century'. He was also a keen mountaineer. In his book Hammarskjöld described his diplomatic activities as an 'inner journey': he is now considered to have been a leading Christian mystic.)

There are lime-loving alpine plants on the slopes of the marble quarry, and the view south towards the mountains, with the torrential stream in the foreground, is inspiring. The summits to the south are called the Abisko Alps in local folklore (the name probably comes from a guidebook about Abisko written in 1914 by Otto Sjögren, in which he speaks about the 'wonderful alpine chain in the Abisko valley'). To the west, on the slopes of Slåttatjåkka, one can easily see dark patches of pines with gnarled ancient trees. Pine also grows relatively profusely around Njakajaure.

The Trail continues southwards from the marble quarry, passing through an increasingly lush birch forest. As far as Nissunjohka, long boardwalks have been laid out, and it is a rare experience to walk uninterrupted on the boards through the rich vegetation. Alternating with the birch, there are dense clumps of Grey Alder (*Alnus incana*) here. The path next reaches a large alluvial cone with waterborne sediments and gravel: the cone formed when the stream branched out in a fanlike fashion with several smaller water-furrows, which the path now crosses. Many of these wet branches are dry during a large part of the summer: the main furrow is crossed by a long suspension bridge. Soon after crossing the bridge you will reach a prepared campsite and a barbecue (within the National Park camping is only allowed on the official sites).

Here, before continuing along the Trail, it is a good idea to go down to Abiskojåkka to look at the waterfalls. The stream forms a beautiful stepped fall, with the north side of Giron providing a formidable backcloth. About 1.5km beyond the bridge across Nissunjohka, just before the next watercourse, Ballinjohka, the Trail meets an old transport route from the 1930s which linked Abisko East and the Sjangeli mines to the west. The track was made as a route for tractors and can now be used as an alternative route to this point, but you would then have to negotiate a ford where the track crosses Nissunjohka. Alternatively you can avoid the ford and walk a good kilometre downstream to the *Kungsleden* bridge. Nowadays reindeer herders drive their four-wheel drive vehicles along the transport route, the tracks from these vehicles also being visible along our Trail.

Now cross Ballinjohka on a bridge: from here a path takes off up towards the campsite and Ballinvaggi. Beyond the path junction there are a few short, but steep, inclines, then, just before you reach the lake of Abiskujávri, there is a beautifully situated resting place next to Abiskojåkka, with a shelter, a latrine, waste-bins and a fireplace. Where the Trail reaches the lake, and within view of the path, there is a small Sámi settlement (Gabna Sámi village), with buildings and boats. The lake itself lies in bowl, birch forest cloaking its slopes.

From this point it is only 4km to the Abiskojaure huts, the overshadowing north wall of Giron providing a dramatic backdrop to the lakeside walk. On the Trail, the forest opens up for long stretches where the vegetation consists of open sub-alpine moor with knee-high dwarf birches. This vegetation can be difficult to penetrate, but the well-trodden path makes the going easy and soon the roofs of the Abiskojaure huts come into view to the south-west. But before you reach them, you cross a bridge over the broad Kamajåkka, a river which rises on Unna Allagas, on the Swedish-Norwegian border in the west. Dippers often appear here around the bridge, while at the far end of the bridge there are some beautiful yellow-white dolomitic rocks and lime-loving vegetation, Mountain Avens (*Dryas octopetala*) being particularly abundant.

Abiskojaure huts (490m)

The huts are located close together on an open grassy bank in the birch forest, the forest limiting views, especially to the west where the steep hillside is cloaked in birch. To the south where there is more open country, the view extends far into the Kamajåkka valley, defined by rounded fell ridges. In front of the huts, 5km away, the lone, steep-sided peak of Kartinvare (1154m) is very imposing despite its relatively low altitude. Left of Kartinvare is a narrow valley – the continuation of the Trail. On a clear day you will also be able to see the summit of one of Lapland's highest peaks, Kåtotjåkka (1991m), through this valley, a dreamlike summit high in the sky. Eastwards, the view is dominated by the 600m dark, striking precipice of the Giron.

The two huts here have 53 beds. The larger hut, which looks like a red barn, is an old engineer's house donated to STF in 1907 by the geologist and prominent Kiruna resident, Hjalmar Lundbohm. The smaller, cone-shaped, *kåta* is also available for walkers. Camping is also possible near the huts. Provisions can be bought here, and there is an emergency telephone.

Day excursions

1. The Abiskojaure huts are not in the best position for excursions to local peaks as they are at a low altitude. However, a good trek is possible up the far side of Kartinvare. Follow *Kungsleden* southwards to Garddenvággi, past the short path to the Giron hut, and then walk diagonally up to Kartinvare's south ridge. The summit affords fine views towards the valley basin of Abiskujávri and, westwards, to Unna Allagas and the Norwegian Sorsteinsfjell. To the south is Kåtotjåkka, with a beautiful crest line towards the highest point, and a precipitous glacier. You also stand a good chance of seeing elk grazing down in the birch forest by Kamajåkka.
Distance: 12km. Height gain/loss: ±600m. Time: about 5 hours.

2. Another fine expedition with considerable botanical interest climbs to Boazučohkka (1300m). The best way is to walk 2km along *Kungsleden* towards the Unna Allakas huts. On reaching the Boazujohka brook, follow it steeply uphill through lush meadow and birch forest, passing a notable small waterfall to reach the fell plateau around the Boazojavri lake, an important grazing ground for reindeer.

The plateau is bordered to the north-west by a cliff, which separates the upper nappe strata from the lower rocks. The cliff is marble, and consequently the vegetation is rich, with many species of lime-loving plants. Further up from the lake the climb is initially rather steep, but then eases as you cross patches of snow and some bouldery terrain to reach Boazučohkka's summit, which is a splendid viewpoint. You can see more of the western Abisko fells from here than from Kartinvare, notably Vuoitasrita (1588m) and the bold ridge of Gorsačohkka (1554m), and the inner parts of Kårsavagge with its delta in the valley bottom.

Distance: 12km. Height gain/loss: ±810m. Time: 7–8 hours.

3. To climb Giron (1551m) and its neighbour Tjåmuhas (1743m), start by following *Kungsleden* southwards for about 1km, then start up into the birch forest, heading towards the Giron cliffs. (The name Giron has the same meaning as Kiruna, both meaning 'grouse'.) Do not cross the bridge across Siellajohka: instead, above the forest line, continue diagonally over a boulder-rich meadow and then climb steeply into the Bahpagurra ravine, which has a small stream. Follow the stream up to the pass between Giron and Tjåmuhas. The view from here is breathtaking, particularly down towards the lake in the 'bowl' of Čoamohasriehppi. From the pass there is a 200m climb over easily negotiated bouldery terrain to the summit of Giron.

From the pass, the alternative is to climb Tjåmuhas, a 500m climb. Both summits afford extensive views over the Abisko valley, Torneträsk and the fells further north. From Giron the view towards Abiskujärvi is staggering. From Tjåmuhas (formerly called Siellatjåkko or Somaslaki), which has two summits, the eastern one being highest, you look northwards into a hanging valley: the ice that gouged out the valley has now disappeared. In clear weather the Lofoten Islands can be seen. There are also majestic views towards the mountains to the south and west. Return the same way.

Distance 16–20km. Height gain/loss: to Tjåmuhas ±1250m. Time: 8–12 hours.

4. If you wish to experience the midnight sun (which is not visible from the huts), there is an easily accessible route, using a rock shelf below the cliffs of Giron, the sun being visible from there. The shelf is clearly visible from the huts. Follow *Kungsleden* back towards Abisko for about 1km.

Distance: 6km. Height gain/loss: ±200m. Time: 2 hours.

5. Another interesting nearby destination is the high waterfall on the west side of Giron. The water cascades down like a silver beam into a deep and spectacular ravine, which is visible from *Kungsleden*. It is possible to walk right to the base of the waterfall, which is one of the highest in the Swedish mountains.

Distance: 4km. Height gain/loss: ±200m. Time: 2 hours.

2. Abiskojaure – Alesjaure

Distance: 22km. Height gain/loss: +330m, –40m. Time: 8–10 hours. Strenuous.

On this stage you leave birch forest for a magnificent fell valley landscape with large lakes, and a relatively extensive view. The valley is framed, to the south, by a high, imposing alpine wall. To finish, you can save 4km of walking by getting a boat across Alesjaure.

To start, walk back over the bridge across Kamajåkka, and then continue southwards along the Trail. You first climb gradually up through the open birch forest to reach the bridge across Siellajohka. About 2km before the bridge you will leave the Abisko National Park. The stream ravine cuts deeply into the terrain so there is an airy bridge crossing, then a short steep climb up out of the forest. Now continue up a tedious hill through Garddenvággi. (Just before the climb, you can see Meditation Place 2 on the Dag Hammarskjöld Way.) The compensation for the climb is the fine view back towards Abiskujávri.

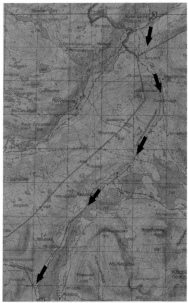

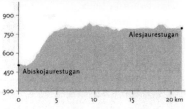

A good kilometre after the bridge, a path takes off towards the Giron hut, which is clearly visible on the other side of the valley. The hut is normally kept locked (you can borrow keys in Abiskojaure or Alesjaure), and is no more than a small square hovel with four beds. But the location is excellent for an overnight stay if you wish to walk through Sillavággi-Ballinvággi to, or from, Abisko. The Trail continues to climb, essentially diagonally, through troublesome vegetation and willow thicket: if it wasn't for the well-trodden path, this would be very hard work, though the stones do make the walking rough and uneven. Soon you pass a large glacial erratic, a good sheltering spot in high winds. If the day is clear, the view ahead of the magnificent massif of Kåtotjåkka keeps the walker's spirits up. When the valley widens and the steep rock face of Kartinvare to the right of the path levels out, you reach a high point. The path is downhill now, reaching a plateau where you pass a small tarn before climbing again to reach a ridge, from where there is an

41

extensive view of the whole valley with its large lakes. You will now also see the high peaks of the Kåtotjåkka massif rise majestically directly from the wide expanses of water in the foreground. Further east another valley opens up between high massifs, and in the background the profile of Alip Vaelivare appears like a whale. To the south you can also see – though you will probably need the help of binoculars – the Alesjaure huts, 10km away in the direction of the lakes. Immediately to the west of the path the fells are low and rounded.

After passing a reindeer fence, which separates the grazing grounds of the Gabna and Leavas Sámi villages, the path approaches the lakeshore. Here it is possible to leave *Kungsleden*: look out between Radujávri and Mieskajávri for a spot where it is possible to wade across so as to continue along a path on the east side of the lakes towards Visstasvággi and Nikkaluokta. But be cautious, wading is difficult unless the water level is very low.

At the northern tip of the lake, in July and August, you can catch a boat from the jetty to the Alesjaure huts. There are usually four boats each day.

As you follow the Trail beside the lake there are good chances of seeing several species of waterfowl. Across the lake, the high precipice of Njuikkostabákti dominates the view, but the landscape is magnificent all the way. At first the shore is brushy – good for the waterfowl – but as the southern shore is approached there are fine sandy beaches. The Trail crosses beautiful meadows, then the stream from Coalmmevággi, to the west, has to be waded, which can be difficult if there is a lot of water. For the easiest crossing, stay close to the lake where the stream divides into numerous rivulets that can be crossed individually: some of them also have plank bridges. Then, at the southern tip of Alesjaure the path leaves the lake, swinging up to the Alesjaure huts, which sit on a small, exposed rocky ridge.

Alesjaure huts (780m)

The huts were moved in 1984 from a site 3km to the south-west when the route of the Trail was changed. At the new site a large collection of huts has now been constructed. There are three overnight huts, with a total of 80 beds, a sauna and a hut with a shop, a communal room and a small exhibition about the local scenery. One hut remains open throughout the year, for safety reasons, with four beds and an emergency telephone. The huts are boldly set between rock faces on a ridge about 20m high. To the south you can see the Aliseatnu river, which meanders through dense willow thickets and, further on, the wide valley of Alisvággi opens out before the view is interrupted by the high summits of the Påssustjåkka massif. To the north the landscape is dominated by the large lakes, with the delta of the Aliseatnu just below the rock. Across Alisjávri you will see the dense collection of tents and small houses of the summer Sámi settlement of Leava. Above the settlement tower the high summits of the Kåtotjåkka and Mårma massifs. There are very good tent pitches on the far side of the bridge over Aliseatnu.

Day excursions
1. The Alesjaure huts are a perfect place for a slightly longer stay, not least because of the high standard of comfort (which, of course, you deserve). In the local area there are plenty of opportunities for different types of day hikes. If you wish to study the fell flora, you can walk up the slopes beneath Alisbuoldda (1285m) where there are meadows with many species and also, remarkably, some very tall plants – for instance an abundance of Garden Angelica (*Angelica archangelica*). Further up, there is a collection of lime-loving plants. Again the reason for this botanical splendour is a layer of marble in the rock strata, separating the upper and lower nappe strata.

The walk can be substantially extended by continuing parallel to the old route of *Kungsleden*, passing the old huts to reach Gungarjohka and then following the stream uphill to Gungarriehppi valley, which has two distinct levels. The valley is very beautiful and interesting, and is one of the rare examples a stepped cirque with paternoster lakes. The two basins are of different geological ages, with a 50m high bedrock threshold between them. In the niches, which have been dug out by small glaciers, there are two lakes, the upper one draining into the lower one, this explaining the name paternoster.

Distance: about 20km. Height gain/loss: ±320m. Time: 6–8 hours.

2. An interesting geological excursion heads for the tundra polygons below the estuary of Unna Visttasvággi, a large, flat area of grass heath, which is covered with a check pattern created by small shallow ditches, which are home to different scrub vegetation. Tundra polygons are formed during a sharp frost when the ground splits into polygons and ice forms in the crevices. When the ice melts, the topsoil drops down. The polygons here were formed in a much colder climate than that of today.

3. For bird watching, an excursion along the shores of Alisjávri (which means 'western lake') is recommended. The area around the lake has many different biotopes, each of which attracts different birds. Around 70 species have been observed in this area, with frequent sightings of Black-throated Diver, Velvet Scoter, Long-tailed Duck, Scaup, Tufted Duck, Goosander and Red-breasted Merganser. Among the rarer species you may come across are Golden Eagle, White-tailed Eagle, Gyrfalcon, Sedge Warbler, Arctic Redpoll and Red-throated Pipit. Rough-legged Buzzards usually breed on the east side of the lake. (For many years a Rough-legged Buzzard pair has nested on the cliff close to the huts.) At its northern end, Alisjávri can be waded at the point where it narrows and joins Radujávri. But the wading is demanding and downright dangerous if the water level is high, and it is safer to cross by boat. Once over, follow, as far as possible, the faint path on the east side of the lake back to the huts. It is also worth seeking out the hidden high waterfall (Phantom Fall) formed by the stream from the Njuikkostakvaggi valley: it is possible to walk behind the water curtain. The fall is situated where the stream makes a sharp bend and is not visible from the path, so you will have to search it out.

Distance: about 15km. Time: 6–8 hours.

4. Mountain excursions are also possible, though it is rather a long way to any of the high summits. Nearby, Durkkechohkka (south-east of the huts) is worth climbing to experience the midnight sun (which is not visible from the huts). A walk to Unna Visstasčohkka (1682m) is also rewarding. Cross the bridge over Alesätno below the huts, then head straight towards the small lakes to the south of Durkkechohkka. The steep climb starts beyond these. To avoid the cliff along the north-west edge of the peak, keep in a straight line towards the highest summit where there are a few snowfields that will come in handy for the descent. The summit is steep, and the view very alpine towards the Påssutjåkka and Mårma massifs. Return the same way.

Distance: about 10km. Height gain/loss: ± about 900m. Time: 5–6 hours.

5. Climbing Påssutjåkka (1935m) is a bigger undertaking, but the effort is rewarded by a very imposing and lonely alpine experience. Follow *Kungsleden* for 2km south from the huts, then turn east for easy walking up towards Unna Visttavággi. At Point 1063, follow the brook ravine up to the lake in the hanging valley below the summit at 1678m, then continue up the relatively modest incline through a boulder field to reach the summit.

The view from there is very dramatic, especially towards the south across the east Bossus glacier and the vertical, rock-vein patterned wall of Sielmatjåkka (1997m). A steep, pointed peak rises from the extended high plateau of Påssustjåkka: a little to the right of this, you will be able to make out the profiles of Sarektjåhkkå, Niak and Áhkká, 80km away. Much closer, the green of the birch forest in Visstasvággi can be seen 1300m straight down to the east. The view westwards is extensive, taking in a long line of distant Norwegian peaks, while to the north-east there is a good general view of the complex Mårma massif.

Distance: about 18km. Height gain/loss: ± 1055m. Time: 10–12 hours.

6. Another big excursion climbs the nameless peak, Point 1835m, in the Mårma massif. Walk past the Alisjávri Sámi settlement and up Njuikkostakvaggi, then go diagonally up the slope through the boulder

sea directly towards Point 1835m. As a viewpoint, it is magnificent, with a dizzy precipice towards the Godu glacier. Return the same way. *Distance: about 20km. Height gain/loss: ± 1055m. Time: 8–12 hours.*

7. A fine viewpoint peak is Gárddečohkka (1507m), to the west. Follow the path towards the Unna Alakas huts, going around Alisbuoldda and then up a steep slope to the summit. There are extensive views towards Norway, Mårma and Påssutjåkka from here. *Distance: about 11km. Height gain/loss: ± 1055m. Time: 5–6 hours.*

3. Alesjaure – Tjäktja

Distance: 13km. Height gain/loss: about +220m. Time: 4–5 hours. Normal.

This stage is relatively short and traverses easy terrain. You follow the wide valley of Alisvággi southwards with high fell tops ahead. The terrain gradually becomes more barren, and the section ends with a relatively steep climb up to the Tjäktja hut.

To start cross Alisaetnu via the bridge below the huts and then walk parallel to the river delta. In the willow thickets and on the water bird-life is abundant. To the north you can see distant Giron and the more pointed summit of Tjåmuhas. As the path continues south, the small peak of Påssusvarasj (1085m) and the steeper Azik (1325m) are landmarks. The path crosses easy scrub heath, peppered with light-coloured flat rocks of quartzite. Before you arrive at the bridge across Bossusjohka, you pass Meditation Place 3 of the Dag Hammarskjöld Way. Before the bridge is reached it is also possible to take a detour south-east, aiming for the Bossus glaciers to make a high alpine, adventurous crossing to the Nallo hut – but this requires glacier equipment. The Trail climbs away from Bossusjohka, circling around Påssusvarasj, after which it remains level as it passes east of the wide

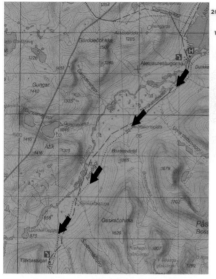

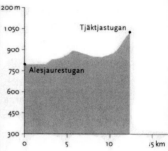

Aliesaetnu river. The old route of *Kungsleden* went west of the stream, and it is still possible to follow that path from the Alesjaure huts, the old wading place across Alisaetnu being wide and usually easy to negotiate.

Ahead now a plateau is framed by mountains on all sides except the north. You ascend slowly from Alisaetnu across meadows and grassy heaths, with easy going underfoot. Now, ahead, you can see the Tjäktja hut high up under the cliff of Muorahisčohkka (1413m). In front of the hut, a steep stream ravine also comes into view. A smaller stream, Sielmmanjira, can usually be crossed without difficulty (early in the season there are often snow bridges here to aid the walker), before the whole height difference of the day's walk has to be negotiated in one gruelling climb up to the bridge across the ravine. The hut is situated about 50m from the bridge.

Tjäktja hut (1000m)

The hut, set immediately below the rocky mountain wall of Muorahisčohkka (1413m), has a marked high mountain character, particularly as snow can remain here for a long time in summer. The view is extensive, especially through Alisvággi. To the north you can see the distant summit of Giron, 30km away. To the east tower the high massifs, for example Gaskačohkka (1629m), while to the south the views are screened off by the high point of the Tjäktja pass. Apart from the tourist hut, there is also a smaller warden hut with emergency telephone and safe storage. There are some tent pitches near the hut.

Day excursions

1. The natural destinations are the peaks to the east, where several summits can be reached without difficulty. To the west there are also exciting places to seek out. Thanks to the limestone veins in the bedrock there is a rich flora on the slope above the hut, and a stroll on the surrounding grassy areas can be rewarding from a botanical point of view.

The summit of Muorahisčohkka (1413m) is the closest, and can be reached without difficulty, taking a straight line directly from the hut. But take care, the rocks can be slippery and have loose gravel on them. Along Alisvággi the peak has a substantial cliff, which is geologically interesting. The summit also offers extensive views towards the high peaks to the east, while towards the west you can see the ice cupola of Riukojietna, one of very few plateau-type glaciers in Sweden. It is possible to return via the south ridge.

Distance: about 4km. Height gain/loss: ±400m. Time: 3–4 hours.

2. It is possible to take a long and arduous trip to Riukojietna, but if you want to walk across the ice, glacier equipment is mandatory. To start with, walk round the northern flank of Muorahisčohkka and then follow the wide valley west towards the Luoktejávrrit lakes. From the west side of these, aim for Point 1190 and carry on diagonally up the hillside below the cliff. From Point 1190 walk due north steeply uphill to reach the 3km^2 glacier. The Norwegian frontier runs over the crest

of the glacial mass, from where a glacial tongue cascades down on the Norwegian side. The view from the crest of the glacier is extensive, the Sarek mountains, 60-70km to the south, being visible. You can walk across Riukojietna and down the eastern tongue to Njivleriehppi, where the glacier has receded substantially. A couple of decades ago the glacier reached all the way to the lake in the valley. Njivleriehppi is a hanging valley, where early glaciers dug out two cirques, one under the other, in which lie paternoster lakes. The lakes function as collecting pools for the glacier silt. The upper lake (1063m) is much more silted up than the lower one (1009m), which is very evident from the difference in the colour of the water. Return to the Tjäktja hut along the same route.

Distance: 20–30km. Height gain/loss: ±500m. Time: 10–14 hours.

3. An excellent nearby viewpoint is Tjäktjatjåkka (1820m) from where you can see almost the whole complex of ridges and precipices of Kebnekaise. The peak is climbed without difficulty along the north ridge, which starts opposite the hut. The climb is only moderately steep to the northern pre-summit, from where the ridge becomes a narrow edge with steep cliffs on both sides. Follow this edge to the highest point. The view from the summit covers a vast area of mountains: the boat-like top ridge of Sielmatjåkka (1997m) is to the north-east, the massive fortress of Räitatjåkka (1934m) is due west, while towards the south-east, behind the precipices of Vaktposten and Knivkammen, you will see Kebnekaise and the 'Wolfback' between the south and north summits. The visible massifs are separated by the Stuor and Unna Reiddavággi valleys. Immediately below the southern precipice of Tjäktjatjåkka lies the second highest lake in Sweden, at 1506m. To descend you can reverse the outward route, or take the west ridge to the Tjäktja pass, continuing back to the hut.

Distance: about 12km. Height gain/loss: ±880m. Time: 5–6 hours.

4.   Tjäktja – Sälka

**Distance: 12km. Height gain/loss: + about 150m, -300m.
Time: 3–4 hours. Strenuous.**

*Today's walk reaches the highest point of Kungsleden, the Tjäktja pass
(1150m). From it there is a steep, demanding descent, but otherwise the terrain
is on the whole easy, and this is a very short section. Early in the season it can
ba hard work plodding through the snow up to the pass.*

It is about 4km and about 150m of climbing from the Tjäktja hut to
the pass to the south. The Trail rises steadily, but snow remains long
into the summer here. The Trail crosses a desolate, flat plateau
surrounded by compact mountains, and soon you will be able to see
the little hut on the highest
point of the pass. The area is a
breeding ground for Ringed
Plover, which you are almost
certain to see. The final climb to
the pass is steep. At the top there
is the shelter and a latrine. It is
often windy and cold here, but

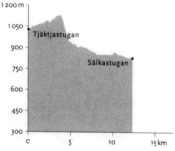

in good weather it is worth pausing, as to the north you can see and follow the route of *Kungsleden* a long way, and enjoy a view of barren, desert-like Alisvággi. To the south there is only a closed wall of mountains, but after continuing for only a few hundred metres, a panorama opens up, with an inviting grassy valley. The south side of the pass is surprisingly steep, and Tjäktjavagge, the valley, forms a wide opening in the high alpine scenery. Tjäktjavagge is an unusual valley as it is long, deeply carved and wide, but also entirely above the treeline. In the far distance, the view is blocked by a characteristic silhouette, the rounded peak of the Stuor Jierta (1543m), but Tjäktjavagge, which is 30km long, continues past this clump, the Trail crossing the full length of the valley.

The surrounding massifs make Tjäktjavagge very inviting. The shape of the peaks on the west side is very different from those on the east side of the river. To the west they are rounded and have flat summits, with steep cliffs falling into Tjäktjavagge and, below the cliffs, a prominent angle along the valley floor, where the grassland abruptly meets the rock. Scree is virtually non-existent. The cliffs on the east side are not as vertical, but, though modest, they merge into high, bold peaks. The mountain wall on the west side of the valley has also been split into cohesive clumps that are separated by deep-cut valleys. The afternoon light often penetrates through these openings, the sun then being reflected on the valley floor. The reason for this unusual west side topography is the constitution of the bedrock. The mountain wall, pushed eastwards by ancient folding, is hard quartzite above a layer of easily crumbling mica schist. There is also limestone between the nappe beds, and this has benefited the spread of the wonderful meadow vegetation, which dominates the west side of the valley. To the east, the vegetation cover is, by contrast, much sparser, and the calmer mountainsides mirror the sloping rock layers, which consist of hard amphibolite from which the highest peaks of the Kebnekaise peaks are made.

From the pass the Trail drops steeply down almost 200m to the valley floor. Before the steepest section starts, you will pass Meditation

51

Place 4 of the Dag Hammarskjöld Way. As you descend, to the west you can see a narrow, interesting valley, which joins Tjäktjavagge at right angles. It is called Geargevággi and leads over a high plateau to the Norwegian border. It is possible to follow the valley, taking a route from the Tjäktja hut to the Hukejaure hut. In Tjäktjavagge the Trail crosses scrub heath and very stony sections, staying close to the river for about 3km. After passing a small lake, the Trail climbs diagonally, parallel to the eastern valley side, the distance from the river increasing as you pass the first opening in the cliffs on the opposite side. This deep cut through the mountain wall can also be used as a route to the Hukejaure hut, but requires wading to cross the river: the river is shallow and it is possible to wade at several places.

It will now be some time before you see the day's finishing point as the Sälka huts lie hidden behind a high ridge. As you near them, look behind for a fine view of the Tjäktja pass below a clearly bow-shaped prominence of rocks. Finally the huts come into view: there is only just over 1km to go now. Continue with a view to the wide valley opening of Stuor Reaiddavággi to the north-east, crossing a bridge to reach the huts.

The Sälka huts (835m)

The huts stand close together, forming a little hamlet on a gravel hill, surrounded by rich meadows where the stream from Stuor Reaiddavággi forms a small delta before it flows into Tjäktjajåkka. This is a wonderful location, with a view of the whole valley and the surrounding peaks. Best of all is the high summit of Tsutsaålkasj (1510m) to the west. Several small streams surround the five huts, which have 54 beds between them. Here you will also find a small shop and a sauna, and an emergency telephone. There are plenty of tent pitches by the huts.

Day excursions

1. The Sälka huts stand at one of the most important intersections in the Kebnekaise area, and are an excellent base for exploration. One of

the most attractive excursions is the climb to Sälka (1865m), the imposing massif to the west, its stand-alone location making the summit a magnificent viewpoint, offering the most extensive panorama in northern Lapland. The main ridges of Sälka form a couple of horseshoes, which enclose two valley basins, separated by an easterly ridge projecting from the main ridge. In both of these valley basins there are glaciers, of which the southernmost, the Sealgga glacier, has a steep ice tongue at the top. It gives Sälka its easily recognisable 'bib' of ice, which hangs down into the impressive eastern precipice.

The peak has two summits, the southern one being the highest, but neither is visible from the Sälka huts. In spite of its impressive proportions, the peak is remarkably easy to climb, especially from the west, though there are extensive boulder fields higher up. From the Sälka huts it is best to walk into the northern basin of the massif, passing a lake at 1050m. The ridge to the south of this lake can be reached by easy wading across Tjäktjajåkka. Aim for a large boulder on the opposite side – as seen from the huts. When the river has been crossed, continue up on the south side of the narrow side valley to gain the lake, from where you carry on steeply and diagonally across grass to reach the east ridge. Followed this westwards up to a pass between the summits. Alternatively it is possible to wade across Tjäktjajåkka further north by a cairn close to the mouth of a tributary stream. Beyond this, follow the north side of the side valley to the lake and wade across the stream by the outlet.

The easiest way to reach the highest point of Sälka from the pass between the summits (at just over 1480m) is to follow the top of the western cliff and then to climb 400m through the boulder field to reach the summit cairn. From the summit the view east is magnificent, taking in the compact and closed alpine world of Kebnekaise. You can also look straight into the east–west valleys that break through the mountain chain – Guobirvaggi, Kaskasavagge and Stuor Reaiddavággi. Among the peaks it is easy to spot Kaskasatjåkka and Gaskkasbákti, which look remarkably sharp. The vertical west side of Kebnekaise is among the grandest mountainscapes in Lapland.

To the west the landscape is very different. Immediately below Sälka are tablelands and plateaux, and in the distance, on the Norwegian side, there are plateau glaciers and a number of needle-sharp peaks. Stetinden, one of the most famous peaks in Norway, can be easily made out thanks to its abruptly chopped off chimney-like summit.

On the way back to the hut, you can follow the south ridge line of the massif to Tsutsaålkasj (1510m) to avoid reversing the outward route. The ridge becomes relatively narrow and has steep cliffs on either side, but you will soon reach the bowl of the Sealgga glacier and, further on, walk through Mielkerriepphi to return to the huts.

Distance: about 15km – the different return routes are approximately the same distance. Height gain/loss: ± about 1000m. Time: 8–10 hours.

2. To the east of the huts there are several interesting, and relatively near, peaks all of which can be climbed without difficulty. A peak offering extraordinary views is Čeakčahjälmen (1906m), a name composed of a combination of Sámi and Swedish words. It is a beautifully rounded peak, seen from the west, but on the opposite side it is finished off with an abrupt cliff to the Reaidda glacier. The peak is best reached from the ravine to the south, between Čeakčahjälmen and Gaskasnjunni. Steep boulder terrain in the lower part gives way, higher up, to a rather narrow and rocky ridge with a modest gradient, though you will have to scramble over flat rocks and past projecting rocks to reach the bouldery summit and the brutal cliff to the glacier. As you climb, the view expands west towards the Sälka massif, which is shown to full advantage from this angle. Most impressive from the summit cairn is the narrow peak of Knivkammen (1878m). The whole line of bold summits in the Kebnekaise massif can also be made out.

Distance: about 8km. Height gain/loss: ±1000m. Time: 5–6 hours.

3. In terms of view, Vaktposten (1852m) is comparable to Čeakčahjälmen. It is a curious mountain, changing shape dependent on where you view it from. Seen from Stuor Reaiddavággi, the fell is a large hump: from the western part of the Reaidda glacier it has a

remarkably modest gradient; while from the Unna Räita hut the profile is a bold ridge with turrets and pinnacles. The summit is most easily reached via the ridge along the Reaidda glacier, and the view is at least as magnificent as that from its neighbours. The summit of Kebnekaise can be made out to the south-east.

Distance: about 12km. Height gain/loss: ± 900m. Time: 6–8 hours.

4. Point 1398, north of the Sälka huts, is usually called 'Sugar-loaf' and is a beautiful little spire with a steep cliff towards Stuor Reaiddavággi. Walk diagonally up its west side: from the top you can continue to a higher peak (1580m) further north. Both peaks provide a good general view of Tjäktjavagge.

Distance: about 10km. Height gain/loss: ± about 900m. Time: 6–8 hours.

5. The Sälka huts are also an excellent base for botanical excursions. Thanks to the lime-rich bedrock to the west of Tjäktjajåkka, the lush meadows are home to many plant species. You can, for instance, easily find Mountain Avens (*Dryas octopetala*), Purple Saxifrage (*Saxifraga oppositifolia*), Rock Speedwell (*Veronia fruticans*) and Lapland Rhododendron (*Rhododendron lapponicum*). At a slightly higher altitude you will also find Cassiope (*Cassiope tetragona*), Pink Lousewort (*Pedicularis rosea*) and Arctic Bellflower (*Campanula uniflora*). To make an excursion here you will have to wade across Tjäktjajåkka first and then stroll around below the cliffs. The lake at 1050m in the side valley opposite the huts can be a pleasant destination for this trip. The stream from the lake forms attractive waterfalls as it drops towards the main valley. The lake itself is a hidden pearl, set in a beautiful hollow surrounded by high peaks. If you wish to spend the night in solitude, it is worthwhile finding a tent pitch in this unforgettable landscape.

Distance: about 8km. Height gain/loss: ± 400m. Time: 4–6 hours.

6. The only boulder glacier in Sweden is situated to the north of the Sälka summit. Wade across Tjäktjajåkka and walk northwards along the valley below Point 1484m, and continue into the side valley north

of this. Follow the side valley westwards for about 4km, passing a few small lakes beautifully situated below the hill meadows. Then, after passing the upper lake, the terrain suddenly becomes barren, dominated by boulders and gravel. Here the front of the boulder glacier appears in the form of a 5m high, bow-shaped wall of large stones. The glacier comprises boulders and soil, with ice-filled cavities. The whole formation is over 600m long and extends up the mountainside towards the north summit of the Sälka massif. The boulders lie in bow-shaped ripples, evidence that the glacier is moving, though much more slowly than an ordinary glacier.

Distance: about 12km. Height gain/loss: ±400m. Time: 4–6 hours.

5a   Sälka – Singi

Distance: 12km. Height gain/loss: about -100m. Time: 4–5 hours. Easy.

The Royal Trail continues south through the ever wider Tjäktjavagge. In spite of the open character of the valley, there is a tangible closeness to the high Kebnekaise massif, and after a short distance you acquire a majestic view towards the Rabot glacier and the highest mountain in Sweden. Towards the south lies Stuor Jierta, a real eye-catcher. Several other routes link with this section of the Trail.

Immediately beyond the Sälka huts you cross a wooden bridge, and continue along Tjäktjajåkka. There are a few pools beside the path, which undulates gently over small gravel heaps. About 500m from the huts the highest summit of the Sälka massif becomes visible for the first time. In the valley, grassy vegetation dominates, but the higher ground on your side of the river is mostly covered by thickets and the path is less distinct as it heads towards the reindeer fence south of the Gaskkasjohka stream, walkers choosing their own routes. As a consequence, it is easy to miss the main path, especially for those walking north. Gaskkajohka splits into numerous brooks running

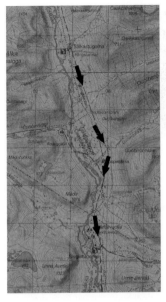

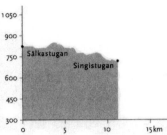

between ribbons of rubble, but these are crossed by wooden bridges. But before these bridges are reached, walkers have the option of following Gaskkajohka up into Kaskasavagge, detouring from the Trail. Far into this valley the sharply pointed Nijbás can be seen. On the other (west) side of Tjäktjavagge, below Mielkeriehppi, there are beautiful examples of landslide 'ripples', a series of half-moons in the steeply sloping green meadows.

After passing the reindeer fence, which stretches right across Tjäktjavagge (forming the boundary between the Leavas and Norrkaitum Sámi village lands), you walk slightly uphill to reach a fork in the path. Here, where the path to Hukejaure heads off is Meditation Place 5 on the Dag Hammarskjöld Way. Rusjka (1706m) can be seen to the south-west here, looking like an upturned boat. It is a beautiful peak and will remain in view for the rest of the day. The Trail now descends to reach the bridge across Guobirjohka.

If you wish to walk east into the Guobirvaggi valley, a worthwhile detour, follow the path before the bridge. Once into Guobirvaggi, you will see three distinctive peaks. To the left is Gaskkasbákti (2043m), high and steep; in the middle, the slender Drakryggen (the Dragon's

57

Back, 1821m), while to the right is Vargryggen (the Wolf's Back) and the south summit of Kebnekaise (2104m), a massive fortress.

On the Trail, Guobirjohka has cut a narrow canyon at the point where it is crossed by a bridge, but downstream it widens into a delta as it approaches Tjäktjajåkka. The bridge is an excellent place for a rest stop, though you might wish to continue for another kilometre to reach the Kuoperjåkka shelter where there is a latrine. From the unusually large shelter you get a good view of the Tjäktjajåkka delta, with its grass-covered islets. You can also see Kuopertjåkka (1914m) in the Guobirvaggi valley. The Trail now heads slightly downhill over mildly undulating terrain, passing the small rills of Singijohkka to reach a path fork.

If you are aiming for Kebnekaise fell station, there is a shortcut here, following the path below Singijčohkka. This path rises steeply to a lake at 979m, where there is good camping and a magnificent view over Tjäktjavagge and the peaks in the west. From the lake you cross a pass, and follow a long descent to reach the path between Singi and Kebnekaise to reach the fell station.

Before continuing from the path fork, turn to admire the full length of Tjäktjavagge. Now follow the Trail, which climbs, then descends to reach a bridge across Tjäktjajåkka. The bridge is situated where the river cascades down into a rock canyon: a beautiful spot. If you cross the bridge you can follow an uncairned route through Neasketvággi to the Hukejaure hut. The Singi huts, our objective, are still hidden behind a small rocky ridge. Do not cross the bridge: instead, walk past it, the Kårtjevuolle summer settlement of the Norrkaitum Sámi village soon coming into view. The settlement is a small collection of buildings close to the beautiful delta of Tjäktjajåkka. A little further on you will see, for the first time, the Singi huts, reached by a final 2km walk along a stony path.

The Singi huts (720m)
This group of huts lies in the middle of the valley on a slope just above the Tjäktjajåkka delta.To the south-west, on the other side of the river

is the sheer cliff of Unna Avrrik (1323m). Four big mountains dominate the surrounding panorama: Rusjka (1708m) lies to the west, with Stuor Jierta (1543m) to the south. To the south-east, in the distance, is Liddubákti (1759m), while the view east is interrupted by the mountain wall of Singičhokka (1704m). Looking north, the view is obstructed by the rocky ridge above the Kårtjevuolle Sámi settlement: consequently, none of the Tjäktjavagge valley is visible that way. In a complete contrast, the view southward along the valley is open, with high peaks far beyond its U-shaped profile. The site consists of three huts with a total of 46 beds, and an emergency telephone. The terrain nearby is poor for camping.

Day excursions

1. The peaks around the huts are tempting destinations. Stuor Jierta is the nearest of these: to reach its summit follow *Kungsleden* south for about 3km, as far as the fork where the path from Láddjurvaggi, to the east, joins the main path. From here, aim straight for the summit cairn, threading a path through the bouldery terrain. The view from this easily reached summit is considered by many to be the best from any vantage point close to the Trail. The east side of the mountain forms a precipice, and from the summit there is a dizzying view down towards the plateau and the many lakes between Stuor Jierta and Liddubákti. Behind rugged Liddubákti and the whale-like ridge of Singičohkka, Kebnekaise can be seen. Westward the eye is drawn to the unusually free-standing massifs of Rusjka and Sälka. To return to the huts, reverse the outward route.
Distance: about 10km. Height gain/loss: ±820m. Time: 4–5 hours.

2. Plateau-like Madir (1078m), on the other side of Tjäktjajåkka from the huts, is also a relatively close objective. The peak, which has a number of awkard precipices along its southern edge, has a rich flora. To explore this flora, cross the bridge over the Tjäktjajåkka and walk below the cliffs, heading west. The meadow here is a good habitat for lime-loving plants, e.g. Mountain Avens, Net-leaved Willow (*Salix*

reticulata) and Lapland rhododendron. To extend the walk, head towards Madirjávri lake, which is set in a high plateau. The view from it, out across Tjäktjavagge and the surrounding peaks is extremely good. To return to the huts, reverse the outward route.

Distance: about 15km. Height gain/loss: ± about 300m. Time: 4–6 hours.

3. A shorter botanic excursion heads for the southern cliff of Unna Jierta, to the east, where the meadows are lime rich and contain many plant species. This short walk is suitable for an evening excursion.

4. Climbing Rusjka (1708m) involves a long and strenuous hike. First walk north to reach the bridge across Tjäktjajåkka, cross and head west into Neasketvággi, where the valley stream will need to be waded. As the east and north side of the peak are very steep, it is best to walk up the western face, reached via the pass between Rusjka and Unna Ruskkas. The view from the summit is similar to that from Sälka, the eye drawn towards Kebnekaise. Return along the outward route, or, as an alternative, walk south and then cross the Báttaláhku plateau down into Neasketvággi.

Distance: about 20km. Height gain/loss: ±1000m. Time: 10–12 hours.

5. Liddubákti (1759m) is another tempting destination, but the walk to it is long and difficult. The ridge visible from the Singi huts is narrow and involves some exposed climbing. From the east, however, it is easy to reach the summit. First follow the path towards the Kebnekaise fell station as far as Lassajávri, then aim for the Liddujávrit lakes, which can be passed along their northern shores, thus avoiding the necessity of wading further on. After passing the peak's south-west wall, which is beautifully sculpted by slip gullies, you climb across bouldery terrain to reach the pass between Liddubákti and Skárttoaivi.

From the summit there is a rarely observed view of the Kebnekaise massif. There is actually an even better view of it from Skárttoaivi (1744m), which can also be climbed on the walk, either as an objective, or by returning to the pass and climbing to Skárttoaivi's high point from there. From the summit, the famous peak of Duolbagorni (1662m), to the north, is completely dwarfed by Kebnekaise. To return to the huts, reverse the outward route.

Distance: about 30km. Height gain/loss: ±1000m. Time: 12–14 hours.

6. The Singi huts can also be a starting point for a climb to Kebnekaise's summit, at 2104m. The ascent starts from Singivággi, from where you take the narrow valley ravine under Guobirčohka. The valley, popularly called Kaffedalen – 'coffee valley' – links to the 'West Path' (Västra Leden) from the Kebnekaise fell station. In Kaffedalen – which was used as the approach to Kebnekaise during the third ascent, in 1895 – there is often a lot of permanent snow. The West Path, which you meet in the upper part of the valley, is obvious when reached, a real trail through a boulder field: follow this trail up the hillside to reach the shoulder of Kebnekaise opposite Vierranvarri (1711m) and continue to the summit huts, and from there press on to reach the South Summit (2104m), following the red-painted stones. On the way back you may wish to follow in Charles Rabot's footsteps along the west ridge. Rabot was the first person to climb the peak, in 1883.

The west ridge narrows as it descends to a pass (Rabot Pass), from where Rabot climbed the peak, having tackled the glacier below, which is also named for him. The cliffs of the west ridge form a dangerous precipice along the entire length above the glacier: take great care, especially if the visibility is poor. The best way to return to the Singi huts from here is to continue past Guobirčohkka and down to where Singivággi meets Tjäktjavagge. Now head south, below the cliffs of Guobirčohkka, to regain the huts.

Distance: 25km. Height gain/loss: ±1400m. Time: 12–14 hours.

Side-tracks from the Royal Trail

5b. Singi – Kebnekaise

Distance: 14km. Height gain/loss: +120m, -150m. Time: 5–7 hours. Normal.

Most hikers on the northernmost parts of Kungsleden end or start their walk in Nikkaluokta. If you wish to do this, you will have to leave the Trail at the Singi huts. From there the walk is along an easy path, involving only limited climbing as it takes in the full length of the Láddjurvaggi valley (the Sámi can be translated as 'Haymaking Valley'). The western section of the valley is deeply cut between high cliffs, but in the central section the valley broadens, becoming even wider, and fertile, in the east where the valley sides also level out. The Kebnekaise fell station is situated in this part of the valley.

Leave the Singi huts and walk towards the sharp edge of Liddubákti. About 1km from the huts the heath is rich in flora: look out for Mountain Avens here. The path now climbs to reach the long and narrow Lassajávri lake. Beyond, the path climbs again, reaching a pass at 840m. From the pass there is a beautiful view towards the peaks to the west, behind you: Rusjka, Unna Jierttas, Unna Avrrik and Stuor Jierta. Ahead the almost 1000m hillsides and cliffs are equally captivating. On the south side of the valley small streams cascade like silver lines down the rock faces, while the face of Liddubákti shows beautiful bedrock strata that descend abruptly and trough-like, a formation geologists call anticlinal. Singičohka, on the north side, is not so vertical, but still impressively high. Follow the path, which is now rough and undulating, past the lake system on the valley floor to reach a collection of large, brown boulders with a metallic lustre due to magnetic pyrite. On the hillsides there are more rusty brown rocks due to iron sediments. The valley narrows here, the path going over a crest and then descending as it bends around Singičohka before levelling out. As the path heads into the wide part of Láddjurvaggi the

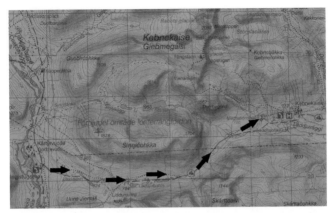

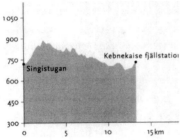

walking becomes very pleasant, with the 1000m cliff of Skárttoaivis hanging literally above the walker. To the north the immense mountain wall of Duolbagorni is now visible: from here the wall is finished off by a slender rock tower. The valley floor is now as flat as a dance floor, reinforcing the feeling of the steepness and height. To the right of the peak the south summit of Kebnekaise can be seen.

The path now climbs from the 'dance floor', passing a beautifully formed round flat slab marked with the striations of ancient ice. This is Meditation Place 6 of the Dag Hammarskjöld Way. Cross Kittelbäcken (Kettle Brook) on a bridge and look for the famous profile of Duolbagorni, with its crater-like niche below the summit. Now climb diagonally to reach the Kebnekaise fell station, which lies hidden behind Kaipak Rock (772m).

63

Kebnekaise Fell Station (690m)

This station lies almost 20km into roadless country, situated below the 'house rock' of Kaipak (the name means 'overhanging mountain wall'). Surprisingly, the South Summit of Kebnekaise is not visible from here. On the other hand you can see Duolbagorni with its imaginary crater, and from the top of Kaipak it is possible to see the whole of Láddjurvaggi and with its famous bastions – Singičohka, Skárttoaivi and Duolbagorni.

The first building was constructed here in 1907, using locally found stones. This building was later extended, and it still forms a part of the principal station building. In this old section, the walls have a patina dating from the infancy of tourism. Later several more buildings were added: today the fell station consists of the extended principal building with a restaurant and communal room, and three free-standing annexes with 190 beds.

There is also a payphone and a shop selling food supplies and hiring high fell equipment. There are tent pitches on the slope towards Kaipak, and further west on the other side of the hill topped with a TV mast. For campers there is a service building with showers, sauna and a kitchen. Yet another building with hotplates is open all year. During the tourist season fell guides are available to conduct visitors to Kebnekaise's summit. Glacier walks and climbing expeditions can also be arranged.

Apart from Route 5, each of the routes below is covered by Lantmäteriet Högfjällskartan map *Kebenekaise* at a scale of 1:20,000. Carrying this map is highly recommended.

Day excursions

1. Climbing Kebnekaise is a cherished dream for many, and no destination can seem more obvious for a fell walker. There are two routes to choose from at the fell station. The West Route is long and laborious, but not very exposed, but the other, the East Route (Østra leden) is more direct, but also more open to the elements and includes

Looking north-west from Stuor-Jiertá

Looking across Lake Laitaure, towards Rapadalen (the Rapa Valley)
in the Sarek National Park

Darfalajohka, with Singičohka on the left and Duolbagorni on the right

Waterfall on the west side of Giron

The Abisko River

The Sälka huts and Čuhčaðalgi

Looking from Čeakčahjälmen towards Knivkammen and the Reaiddá glacier

The Rabot glacier and Kebnekaise from the west

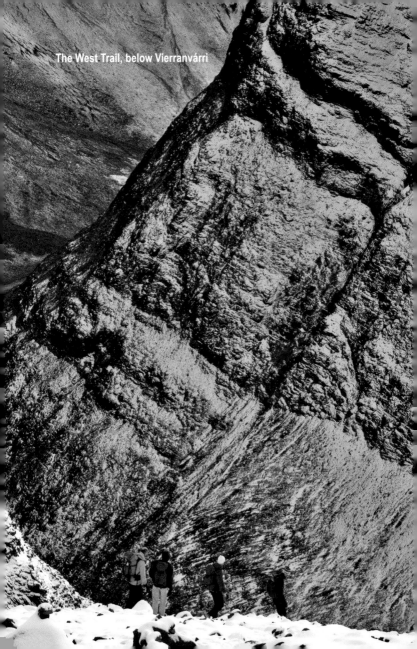

The West Trail, below Vierranvárri

Looking eastwards from Laddjurvággi in late August

Above Padje Kaitumjaure, with Livamčohkka on the right.

Opposite above Evening sun behind Nieras, from Saltoluokta.

Opposite below Looking towards Suottasjtjåhkkå on the left and Niják on the right, in Sarek. In the foreground is the Akkajaure reservoir.

The Laitaure delta from Nammasj

elica archangelica

Andromeda polifolia

Saxifraga aizoides

llodoce caerulea

Salix reticulata

Sedum rosea

champsia alpina

Mountain Burnet Moth

Trollius europaeus

Skierffe from Aktse

some climbing. If you have problems with exposure, the East Route is not a good choice.

The West Route starts up Kitteldalen, heading west from the fell station on a path towards Duolbagorni, then going up the small ravine south of the summit. The path is marked with cairns and easy to follow. At the top of the ravine there is a magnificent hollow surrounded by sheer cliffs. The valley stream, Kittelbäcken, can be easily forded high up in the valley. One landmark that attracts attention is the long snow gully on Vierranvárri (1711m), a peak that used to be called 'Rullevara' after an early climber named Rudolf Berg, whose nickname was *Rulle*. Ironically, Berg has no real claim to a place in Swedish mountain history, but happened to be with a more famous climber, Natte Flygare, in 1901. The two made the fourth recorded ascent of Kebnekaise, and since *rulle* means 'rounded' in Sámi, the name stuck. The peak has a vast boulder field that has to be negotiated: walk straight towards the pass (1440m) to the south of Vierranvárri, the walking usually being across a steep snowfield. Glacier Crowfoot (*Rananculus glacialis*) grows close to the pass, a glimpse of that being one reward for attaining the pass. Another is the dizzying view down into Singivággi. From the pass an alternative climb reaches the summit of Duolbagorni – an easy ascent of just over 200m. But the real prize is reached by continuing along the West Route, heading north from the pass up to the summit of Vierranvárri, from where the view offers outstanding depth perspectives and silhouette effects into the narrow cleft of Singivággi and Láddjurvaggi beyond. Unfortunately from here there is a marked loss of height, as you have to walk down to the pass north of Vierranvárri at 1520m. From this second pass you will see a narrow valley towards the west: that is Kaffedalen (see Section 5A, Day Excursion 6 above). Now follow the well-trodden path through the boulder fields up on to the southern shoulder of Kebnekaise to reach the summit huts. They are about 100m apart and are the highest buildings in Sweden (at 1880m). The newer of the huts dates from the early 1960s, but the older one, which has been recently smartened up, is the more attractive of the two. The huts are open all year and provide a primitive overnight facility. Posts have been placed between the huts, something to remember if the mist comes down. It is a good idea to have a rest by one of the huts, and even to leave your rucsac there before the final climb to Sweden's highest point.

To finish, walk up and across the summit plateau of Kebnekaise. Above this rises the summit, which is actually a glacier, 40–50m thick and shaped like a great white pyramid, the last few few metres of climbing being a snow plod. This is the crown of the country's mountains, a 2000m summit with ice and white snow on black rock. The South Summit is really iconic – a snowy peak surrounded by dizzying spaces. Because of the snow, the highest point in Sweden is not solid land, and its altitude has varied over the years. On the map it is now stated to be 2104m, but the average during the last 20 years has been higher and in winter the altitude is always a few metres higher. The North Summit of Kebnekaise (2097m) is the highest point of the country on solid land.

The view from the South Summit is in a class of its own. According to reports, around 40,000km², 8% of the area of Sweden, can be seen, if the visibility is good. With the help of binoculars, many peaks can be identified, even distant ones such as Storsteinsfjell in the Narvik area. Much closer is an alpine landscape with a wild and complex topography of precipices and glaciers, and a wilderness of untouched valleys. This combination of dramatic and undeveloped country is the most prominent characteristic of Sweden's mountains and is rarely as convincingly seen as from the South Summit.

To the south the view is of a wide expanse of high peaks and plateaus with, in the far distance, the mountain world of Sarek. Only to the east does the panorama from the summit have a different character. Here the dark hues of forests and flat land formations dominate.

The summit glacier is a narrow ridge, which merges into cliffs above the Rabot Glacier to the west, and the Björling Glacier to the east. The ridge continues towards the North Summit, but going that way demands crampons, familiarity with ice walking and an ability to negotiate very exposed routes: you must be an experienced climber in order to continue. To return to the fell station, reverse the West Route: the snowfields in Kitteldalen are excellent for sliding down, but be careful as they can be treacherous with hard ice as well as snow.

Distance: about 24km. Height gain/loss: ±1620m, including ±200m to Vierranvari. Time: 10–12 hours.

2. The East Route is a shorter route to the South Summit. It is therefore more frequently used by climbers, but as Emmerich Rossipal writes in his classic guide *Kebnekajsfällen* (*The Kebnekaise Mountains*), 'In all conditions, the fell walker here encounters a terrain of a different kind and steepness from that which one usually experiences during the climb to a fell summit'. The route involves both a glacier traverse and some sections of modest rock climbing. It is not recommended for inexperienced people unless they are accompanied by a guide. But for those used to glaciers and climbing it is rarely a problem to follow the route independently. But take care: difficult weather conditions, such as fog freezing on the rock, can make the route very dangerous.

Follow the path from the fell station towards Duolbagorni. On the slopes below Kebnetjåkka, the vegetation is in places prolific, with, occasionally, unusual species: Northern Catchfly (*Silene uralensis*) can be found here. When Jökelbäcken (a conspicuous stream – but one of several, generally the fourth crossed on the walk, but the number may vary with weather conditions, so check your position on the map) is reached, turn north up into the ravine it has carved. The stream in the ravine can easily be forded close to the 1050m contour, from where there is a steep, hard climb up 'Storbacken' (the great hill), one compensation being the Moss Campion (*Silene acaulis*), Slender and Alpine Gentian (*Gentianella tenella* and *G. nivalis*) that grow here. The ravine emerges at the small glacier below the summit of Kebnetjåkka (1763m). On the plateau above the glacier the gradient of the climb decreases, and the tall mountain walls of Kebnekaise, which have not been visible so far, come into view. The plateau is a remnant from 70 million years ago, when the chain of mountains was eroded after being uplifted by earth movements.

Continue across boulder fields to reach the ice tongue of the Björling glacier that faces Kitteldalen. When on the ice, look out for crevasses beneath the snow and if there is a well-trodden track, follow it. The glacier crossing ends on the often snow-clad dragon-back ridge that extends right up to rock face below the summit plateau of Kebnekaise. The ridge is usually icy, and will have crevasses hidden under the snow. At the rock face, the climb starts with an airy traverse of the Gudjohnsen's Shelf, which goes 200m northwards above the Björling glacier. (The shelf is named for the Danish doctor Th. S. Gudjohnsen, who was the first person to follow it in 1920.) There are paint marks on the rock, and the lichen is worn away, so the route is easy to find, but care is needed: at times the shelf slopes outwards, and loose stones call for increased vigilance. However, the climbing is straightforward. The very rare Arctic Poppy (*Papaver radicatum*) grows here, on the few patches of earth: please observe it from the shelf as climbing to reach it is very dangerous.

At the end of the shelf, climb straight up the rock face using the southernmost of two clefts. There are fixed ropes for aid and security, and the climbing is easy, but care is needed. The cleft leads onto the summit plateau of Kebnekaise. As you reach this the older summit hut comes into view. Finally, about 240m from the hut you will reach the South Summit. Most people return along the same route, but it is, of course, possible to take the West Route. If taking the East Route down, be careful on the Storbacken. The snowfields here are popular chutes, but sometimes there is ice in the snow and it is then easy to lose control.

Distance: about 16km. Height gain/loss: ±1420m. Time: 8–10 hours.

3. Kebnetjåkka (1763m) is an excellent summit viewpoint at a lesser altitude which can be easily reached by walking straight up the slope above the fellstation. This direct route reaches the plateau below the summit: continue up to the summit where there is a radio mast. Because of the peak's central position in the Kebnekaise massif, the views from here are tremendous. During the descent to the fell station

you can take advantage of several snowfields, which usually remain on the south slope right through the summer.

Distance: about 10km. Height gain/loss: ±1070m. Time: 4–5 hours.

4. For friends of glaciers, a trail across the large icy mass of the glaciers appears tempting. The possibilities are many, but a word of warning is necessary: the glaciers of Kebnekaise are full of crevasses and are definitely not to be treated lightly. Many accidents have taken place. To make this excursion, there is an unconditional safety rule that you walk with at least two other persons tied into a rope. Travelling that way, a glacier traverse to Tarfala can be carried out relatively safely.

Follow the East Route to the Björling glacier, where you should rope up before continuing across the glacier near Kebnetjåkka towards the pass below the North Summit of Kebnekaise. The central part of the glacier is often bare and covered in moraine (stones and gravel). At the pass there are many treacherous crevasses, and caution is of utmost importance. On the other side of the pass you encounter the similarly crevassed Storglaciären (the Great Glacier), where you should keep close to Kebnetjåkka, taking care as there is an area of crevasses below the obvious cliff line of the peak. On the lower part of the glacier there are several dangerous glacier wells situated along the midline. From Storglaciären it is best to return to the fell station via the Tarfalavagge route.

Distance: about 18km. Height gain/loss: ±1000m. Time: 8–10 hours.

5. South of Láddjurvaggi, an attractive objective is the ridge leading up to Skárttoaivi (1744m). From the fell station this looks like a high mountain wall, but to the east the gradient is actually reasonable. Walk down to the bridge across Laddjujohka and climb the ridge through an area of large boulders below Point 1293m. This collection of boulders is interesting as it is one of the few examples in the fells of a so-called 'protalus wall'. The boulders have tumbled down from the cliff above and bounced far out from the rock face down on to a snowfield where they have slipped and accumulated into a bank, explaining why the

ridge is situated so far from the cliff. On the slope to the left there are fine alpine meadows with lush vegetation and examples of Lapland Rhododendron (*Rhododendron lapponicum*) and Pallid Milk-vetch (*Astragalus frigidus*). Now head eastwards to circumvent the cliff, then follow a deep ravine to reach a high plateau. Point 1293m is one of the best viewpoints for seeing Kebnekaise from the south. From it, you can cross easy, bouldery terrain to Point 1744m, from where it is possible to see as far as Sarek to the south.

Distance: about 10km. Height gain/loss: ±600m. Time: 4–5 hours.

6. Another interesting destination is the Tarfala valley with its grand scenery and famous research station. Walk east for 2km from the fell station to reach a bridge over Darfalajohka. Cross this and turn left (north) on a path, still through birch forest, into Darfalavággi. The valley is comparatively narrow here, with a line of cliffs on the other (west) side of the river. Eventually you leave the forest: continue until you reach a small building, on the opposite side of the river, where measurements of the river flow are taken. Close by a plaque, fixed to a large boulder, is a memorial to the glaciologist Valter Schytt who was responsible for the building of Tarfala scientific station: the power lines running parallel to the path provide electricity to it. The station was quite modest when initially constructed in 1947 after a site had been chosen by Schytt. The station's purpose was glaciological investigations on Storglaciären. Today there is a modern, comfortable settlement, a small cabin village in the middle of the alpine environment of the valley. Over the years the world's longest continuous record of the variations in the size of a glacier has been produced from here. If the station is manned, there is usually a chance to see a video about the work. Valter Schytt also created, with the glaciologist Per Holmlund, a detailed map of the Kebnekaise massif.

Just over 1km beyond the station is the STF hut by Darfalajávri, set in one of the grandest alpine environments in the Swedish mountains, with glaciers and high summits surrounding the lake.

Distance: 16km. Height gain/loss: ±480m. Time: 5–7 hours.

7. Shorter day excursions are also possible from the fell station. One idea is to look for plants in the slope over towards Kittelbäcken. You could also visit Björngrottan (the Bear Cave – probably named for its use by hibernating bears), a boulder cave set on the 600m contour by the boulder ridge south of Láddjujohka. Another interesting geological sight is the number of kettle holes by Láddjujohka, 1km south of the bridge across Kittelbäcken. These are perfectly polished holes in the rock, formed by the scouring action of stones caught in turbulent water. You can reach them from the Meditation Place by the bridge. The stream here runs through a small rocky canyon with beautifully shaped and polished rocks.

5c. Kebnekaise – Nikkaluokta

Distance: 19km (12km if the boat is taken). Height gain/loss: -220m. Time: 5–6 hours. Normal.

To start, walk eastwards to the bridge across Darfalajohka, and then descend through the birch forest, rounding Darfaloalgi mountain. There is picturesque scenery at Nikkaluokta, particularly westward, with the 'gate' to Kebnekaise, formed by steep and high summits. Before Nikkaluokta you will also pass the large delta at the west end of Laddjujávri lake. The lake itself can be crossed by boat.

This day walk is well frequented and the path is wide. As far as Darfalajohka you walk through sparse and patchy birch forest. At the bridge, where there is a latrine, the river cascades attractively through a deep ravine. Beyond the bridge the walk is through denser birch forest. There is a long downhill section towards Laddjujohka with, behind, views to the Kaipak and the fell station and the eye-catching peaks around Láddjurvaggi. The top section of Gaskkasbákti (2043m) also appears for a short while in a narrow gap to the north through Tarfalavagge. Ahead of you are the low fell plateaus south of

71

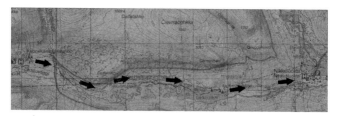

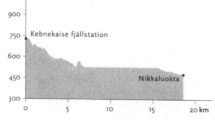

Láddjurvaggi. The trail passes between large boulders below the steep Darfaloalgi (750m): here you will pass Meditation Place 7 on the Dag Hammarskjöld Way.

The forest is here is lush as the cliff above the path is limestone, attracting many lime-loving species such as Tufted Saxifrage (*Saxifraga cespitosa*), Purple Saxifrage (*Saxifraga oppositifolia*), Rock Speedwell (*Veronica fruticans*) and Rock Sedge (*Carex rupestris*).

Beyond Darfaloalgi the terrain undulates as far as the wide river basin of Laddjujohka. The river has built up an extensive delta at the entrance to Laddjujávri lake: since the end of the last Ice Age, silt from the glaciers of the Kebnekaise massif has been deposited in the lake, which has shrunk by half. In the delta there are bogs, tied off lakes, channels and meandering loops: a perfect habitat for water fowl – and definitely for mosquitoes!

At the point where the path reaches the river there is a small landing stage from where you can get a boat to the east shore of Laddjujávri. Using the boat it is possible to cut out 7km of walking along the north shore of the lake. Most walkers take advantage: the boats follow a schedule – look for the timetable. The trip is an experience in itself, especially the ever-changing perspective of the mountains reflected in the watery mirror.

By the east landing stage there is a coffee hut with refreshments. The remaining stretch to Nikkaluokta is very easy going along a path as wide as a tractor track. Immediately beyond the coffee hut, you go over the brow of a hill, where the view behind, westwards, towards Kebnekaise's South Summit and Duolbagorni is very beautiful. To the south the eye is drawn to Stállegorsa, a deep and imposing cleft in the mountain, which was probably chiselled out by an ancient glacier. The hillside south of Láddjurvaggi is scored by almost parallel lines, which demand attention. They are so-called ice edge furrows and were formed by glacier water gushing between an ice tongue in the valley and the hillside, the water etching the furrows. The succession of furrows shows how the ice has shrunk back. Cross Čievrrajohka by bridge to reach excellent resting-places. Soon you will catch your first glimpse of Nikkaluokta – the chapel, beautifully situated on a ridge.

6. Singi – Kaitumjaure

Distance: 13km. Height gain/loss: -120m. Time: 4–5 hours. Normal.

Today's walk leads through a narrow section of U-shaped Tjäktjavagge. The path stays close to the wide and constantly babbling valley stream, then, towards the end of the day, there is a relatively steep descent to arrive in the protected fell birch forest by Padje Kaitumjaure lake. The lake is exquisitely situated below high and precipitous peaks.

From Singi the walk continues across undulating terrain with only some short climbs. Ahead, the view is dominated by loaf-shaped Stuor Jierta (1543m) and the wild, rugged, landslide precipice on Stuor Avrrik (1354m). Behind you, to the north, the views through Tjäktjavagge are limited by the high ridge above the Kuorthevuolle Sámi settlement. Also northward, but a little more west, the Sälka massif is prominent, with a marked 'bib' created by the glacier tongue below the summit.

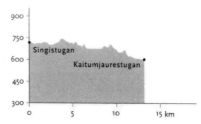

Between Stuor Avrrik and Stuor Jierta the walking is easy, and you will soon reach very flat terrain where Gavgulvaggi opens up to the east. Here there are extensive river deposits from the last Ice Age, with moraine ridges and kame mounds (kames are built up between ice blocks at the edge of a glacier). The path winds through extensive, but low, willow clumps which cover the surface of the deposits. Anywhere along the bank of the Tjäktjajåkka bank is a pleasant place for a rest.

For those with interest in botany, it is worth leaving the rucsac behind for an excursion to the meadow-like slope of Stuor Jierta where the vegetation is prolific, with large areas of Mountain Avens (*Dryas octopetala*) and other lime-loving species, such as Northern Catchfly (*Silene uralensis*). Stuor Jierta can also be easily climbed from this direction (but requires about 4 hours to negotiate the 800m climb up and down).

Further south there is a short ascent, before it is downhill all the way to the bridge across Tjäktjajåkka. Up on the brow before the bridge, look behind: the view northwards extends through Tjäktjavagge as far as the mouth of Stuor Reaiddavággi. To the south, you can let your eyes follow the roller-coaster of *Kungsleden* down to the Kaitum valley and across the high plateau of Muorki, from where

74

the Trail disappears as it descends into the Teusa valley. In the far distance it is possible to distinguish the Sarek summits.

Beyond the bridge there is a comfortable downhill slope to the Kaitum huts, the scenery becoming increasingly dramatic as you first enter the birch forest, which becomes more sparse as you near the huts.

The Kaitum huts (600m)

The landscape here offers genuine contrasts. The valleys of Tjäktjavagge and Kaitum meet here at a 'crossroads' framed by three high peaks. Birch forest covers the valley floor and the hillsides. From the hut location, which is at the edge of the forest, there is a good view over the Kaitum valley and the delta at the west end of lake Padje Kaitumjaure, where elks often graze. On the other side of the delta, there is a summer settlement for Mellanbyn Sámi village. The deeply cut lake extends eastwards into a U-shaped valley between the majestic mountain walls of Livamcohka (1481m) and Leaibečeabetčohkka (1346m). In the opposite direction the terrain climbs steeply up to the third peak, Sánjarcohkka (1580m). The site has two huts and one *kåtor* with a total of 30 beds. Provisions can be bought here, and an emergency telephone is available. There is good camping ground on the open heaths down by the delta.

Day excursions

1. Close to the huts, the canyon of Tjäktjajåkka, just before it runs into Padje Kaitumjaure, is well worth seeing. You can stroll along the cascading river, which runs, in places, between 2m cliffs. The landscape as a whole, with the mountains, the valley, the cleft and the river is a consummate aesthetic experience.

2. The three surrounding fells are tempting destinations for a longer day excursion. The nearest is Sánjarčohkka, which offers a tremendous view, because of its position, right between the mountain worlds of Kebnekaise and Sarek. The climb starts straight from the huts, going

straight up over scrub heath and, higher up, grassland. At about 1000m the grass gives way to a field of small boulders. At the highest point there is a wooden cross and a letter box with a visitors book. The view is dominated by the exquisite Kaitum valley, which from here is perfectly symmetrical, mountain walls enclosing the river. To the north-west, the summits of Kebnekaise are visible, while to the south you can see the chain of summits of Sarek. The range of views is enormous. To return to the huts, reverse the outward route.

Distance: about 6km. Height gain/loss: ±980m. Time: 3–4 hours.

3. Another alternative is a long walk round Sánjarčohkka. Start by taking *Kungsleden* northwards to the bridge across Tjäktjajåkka, where you head off west into Sánjarvággi below the pointed north summit on the peak. The walk continues past Sánjarvággijávri lake, and the larger Viddjajávri lake, at the south end of which you have to cross a field of large boulders. Heading south you reach the Kaitumjåkka valley, which also forms the boundary of the Sjaunja Nature Reserve, which will be of interest to birdwatchers: the small bogs and willow thickets around the stream's small delta is popular with waterfowl and waders. Now follow Kaitumjåkka back to the huts.

Distance: 26km. Height gain/loss: ±300m. Time: 8–10 hours.

4. Livamčohkka can be climbed from the west, having first followed *Kungsleden* south to the bridge across Kaitumjåkka. Immediately beyond the bridge, go diagonally up the steep hillside, heading through bouldery terrain, which starts a low level. Aim for Point 1224m at first, then directly for the summit at 1481m. From there the view is best towards the deep valley by Livanjávri, to the south-east. From the summit you should head north-east for just under 1km to reach the cliff towards Padje Kaitumjaure. From here the giddying view down towards the lake will give you butterflies in the stomach. To return to the huts, reverse the outward route.

Distance: about 12km. Height gain/loss: ±880m. Time: 6–8 hours.

5. To reach the summit of Leaibečeabetčohkka, head north along *Kungsleden* as far as the bridge across Tjäktjajåkka. From there it is a relatively modest climb to the top, from where there is a wild view towards the Kaitum valley and the northern precipice of Livamčohkka. There is a suitable resting place by the little lake in the pass towards the higher, eastern, summit. To return to the huts, reverse the outward route.

Distance: about 18km. Height gain/loss: ±680m. Time 8–10 hours.

7. Kaitumjaure – Teusajaure

Distance: 9km. Height gain/loss: +200m, -300m. Time: 3–4 hours. Easy.

This stage crosses part of Sjaunja Nature Reserve and is one of the shortest along the Royal Trail. It starts across a high plain, the landscape having an open feel, which seems very novel if you have arrived here from the north. High peaks can, though, be seen at various distances round about. The path descends ever steeper towards the stage end, dropping into one of the most beautiful valleys in the mountain world, the Teusa valley.

The day starts with a 1km walk through birch forest, the terrain undulating as far as the bridge across Akitumjåkka, the river

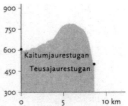

77

forming a boundary of the Sjaunja Nature Reserve. Close to the bridge the river gushes over some powerful, 2m-high waterfalls. The view ahead is dominated by the slope towards the high plain of Muorki, and the peak of Urttičohkka (1203m) which has an unusual long, level rock face. Beyond the bridge the ground is stony, with smooth slate slabs sloping down towards the path. You cross a reindeer fence, after which the forest thins, the Trail continuing over undulating terrain with many small pools in the depressions. As you ascend, the Trail is framed by the rounded Urttičohkka (1203m) and Slieknjamačohkka (1482m). Gradually now, the Trail approaches a flat brow, and the terrain becomes more level, though the going is still stony. As you climb, more and more of the glaciated Sarektjåkka massif becomes visible to the south – the view dominated by the Great and North Summits. Behind you, looking north, there is a beautiful view towards the Kaitum valley and the long and high mountain ridges which succeed each other as a series of silhouettes towards Kebnekaise: between Stuor Jierta and Leaibečeabetčohkka you can see the huge, rugged rock face of Liddubákti.

This walking across the Muorki high plain is very pleasant, with extensive views in all directions. When the Trail starts to descend, you will see another plateau in the distance: the Trail crosses that tomorrow. The Teusa valley now becomes visible, while to the east beautifully shaped Suorregaise (1560m) in Livanvággi provides a feast for the eyes. The walk now starts to descend towards the Teusa valley. Just where the birch forest starts, the stream from Muorki runs over beautiful slate slabs. Here the view across Teusajaure is amazingly grand, the eastern part of the lake lying below steep precipices. Look, too, for a rare concentration of Bog Rosemary (*Andromeda polifolia*), which grows in dense carpets that have a rose-coloured hue when the flowers bloom. The local flora, which is rich close to the stream, also includes Alpine Butterwort (*Pinguicula longifolia*) and Net-leaved Willow. The descent to the Teusajaure huts is very steep, but the view west to vertical rock faces projecting through the forest will take your mind off it until the huts become visible between the trees. By the time you see them you are almost there. Beyond the huts, on the other side of the lake, the curious protuberance in the shore line is where Gáppejåhkkå has deposited gravel and sediment into an alluvial cone split by several water runnels.

The Teusajaure huts (525m)

Embedded in fertile birch forest, near the lake shore, are two overnight huts, a sauna and a warden hut, as well as a locked hut for nature conservancy staff. There are 30 beds in total, and an emergency telephone. Camping is only possible close to the huts.The location by a gravelled headland, where the stream runs into the lake, is one of the most elegant along the Royal Trail. The huts are protected from the weather by the forest, but the site is nevertheless characterised by the dramatic landscape even if the view is limited to the Teusa valley. To the east, the Kårsatjåkka massif tumbles down to the expansive waters of Teusajaure, the lake watched over on the southern side by another high summit, Guolbantjåhkkå (1197m). Opposite the huts, where the Trail continues, the terrain is lower, but westward it rises to Gáppetjåkkå (1457m).

Day excursions

1. The desolate and rarely climbed Kårsatjåkka (1703m) is a tempting destination from Teusajaure. Walk up on to the Muorki plain and head east towards Livanvággi. Aim for the highest point of the high Kårsatjåkk ridge as you walk easily through the scrub. At about the 1000m contour the landscape changes, the walker threading through a sea of boulders. The ridge you are on heads up to a crest interrupted by a cliff leading down towards one of the two small glaciers of the massif. Follow the ridge to reach the summit, from where the view is awesome. To the south is the slightly higher summit of Kuopertjåkka (1730m), part of the same massif, next to which, but 1300m below, is the western end of lake Gágirjaávri, which is situated at the east end of the Teusa valley. To the north mountain ridges succeed each other all the way to Kebnekaise. The best return route is to cross to Point 1668m and Slieknjamačohkka (1482m), so follow the summit ridge

west towards the Teusa valley. From Slieknjamačohkka the view is spectacular, particularly towards the narrowest part of the Teusa valley. *Distance: about 25km. Height gain/loss: ±1180m. Time: 12–14 hours.*

2. You can of course be content with just reaching Slieknjamačohkka, which is a fine viewpoint and a considerably less onerous excursion than that to Kårsatjåkka. An even closer objective is Urttičohkka (1202m), north-west of the huts. To reach it, take a straight line northwards from the forest boundary. The summit offers a comprehensive view towards the western parts of the Teusa valley. *Distance: about 8km. Height gain/loss: ±680m. Time: 3–4 hours.*

3. Gáppetjåhkkå (1457m), on the other side of Teusajaure, is another interesting objective, but it does mean either rowing or getting a lift across the lake, and you will have to force your way through the forest on the other side. *Distance: about 10km. Height gain/loss: ±960m. Time: 6–7 hours.*

8. Teusajaure – Vakkotavare

Distance: 15km. Height gain/loss: +400m, -480m. Time: 4–5 hours. Strenuous.

South of the Teusa valley you reach the Stora Sjöfallets National Park, and the Lule Sámi language area, place names being spelt in this new dialect. The day starts with a boat trip, after which the Trail climbs to a high plateau similar in character to that north of the lake. The climb is strenuous, but the reward is a fine view northwards. Further on, the view expands towards the Sarek peaks. The day finishes with a very steep descent to Vakkotavare in the Stora Sjöfallet valley.

The 1km rowing route across Teusajaure is marked with buoys. There are three boats each equipped with life-jackets. You must count on

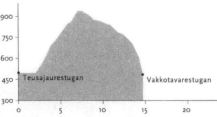

rowing back and forth three times, so that walkers on each side always have a boat at their disposal. In strong winds this is hard work, and you will need to be careful if the lake is very choppy. When the hut warden is on site, you can book a lift with a motorboat. Walkers approaching from the south can request a lift by hanging a plastic can on a mast. Because of the regulated waterflow in the Teusa valley, the lake is shallow close to the shore. The shallow section is relatively wide on the southern side, where Gáppejåhkå almost forms a small delta. In the forest behind the sandy shoreline there is a shelter.

Once across the lake, the first kilometre of walking is along a path through dense birch forest, arriving close to a ravine carved out by Gáppejåhkå. A couple of kilometres futher on there is a ledge by a small brook, which can be used as a bathtub. This is a superb site for camping, with delectable views over the beautiful Teusa valley.

The birch forest ends at about the 650m contour, the Trail then crossing scrub heath with some tall vegetation. On the hillside to the west you can see a reindeer herder's hut, while to the east is Guolbbantjåhkkå (1197m), Several low, twisting eskers now come into view: they were formed in meltwater tunnels within the deep ice of the

81

last Ice Age. Shortly after crossing a stream coming in from the east – it can be easily waded – the Sarek peaks come into view. Many summits can be distinguished, including the north summit of Sarektjåkka (2056m) and Kavapakte (1906m). Behind, to the north, you can study the softly undulating landscape where you have traveresed. Gáppejåhkå is a peculiar mountain from this perspective, a saddle with two high points.

A bridge is used to cross a substantial stream running down from Guolbbantjåhkkå. The stream has carved a ravine, which the Trail twists and turns around before reaching the bridge. (The old route of *Kungsleden* still exists here, but it heads uphill to reach a wading point: the bridge is clearly the better option.) Beyond the bridge the Trail heads towards Råhpatjårro fell (1677m), a drawn-out climb being required to cross the crest. Ahead now you will see an undulating plateau with meltwater deposits and, as a backdrop, an even better view of Sarek with its chain of spiky peaks. The ice fall of the Suottasjiegna glacier can be seen, together with Nijak (1922m), which stands beside the high bulk of Ahkka (2015m). You will also see Suorvajaure lake, the next objective.

The view is phenomenal, and as the walking is now easy can be thoroughly enjoyed. The vegetation is dominated by low grasses and shrub heaths, but there is also a confused heap of large boulders, which gives the area a peculiar appearance. Cross some easily waded streams and continue past the striking Våkkuakvárátja (874m), to the west. When the Trail reaches birch forest, the land drops steeply away. The descent here is the most strenuous on the Royal Trail, but is thankfully short. As you descend, the view towards Suorvajaure expands: the lake is a reservoir and the view can be marred by the ugly shoreline if the water level is low. At the bottom of the steep climb is the Vakkotavare hut.

Vakkotavare hut (440m)

The hut is located by the Ritsem road, and the buses using the road stop just outside. Although the hut is embedded in the forest, there are fine views from the porch. The hut, which does not have any safe storage, has 16 beds. It is only open during late winter/early spring, that is from middle of March until the end of April, and then during the summer from July to September. At the hut the Royal Trail is interrupted, beginning again at Saltoluokta, 30km east along the road and across the lake. Not surprisingly, walkers use the bus, which is timed to connect to the ferry beyond Vietas for the lake crossing to Saltoluokta.

SALTOLUOKTA –

Distance: about 73km. Height gain/loss:

From Saltoluokta four easy and varied day walks pass through a landscape that has a different character from that north of Vakkotavare. There the Trail is in a genuine high mountain, alpine area, whereas south of Saltoluokta it meanders through a borderland between the steep summits of Sarek, to the west, and the forested country to the east. On your four days you will become familiar with both mountain heaths and coniferous forest.

The first day walk to the Sitojaure lake is also the longest. Immediately beyond the Saltoluokta fell station there is a steep climb through birch forest to open fell heath, offering easy walking and extensive views. The path continues southwards through a wide valley with a big rock face to the west. Towards the end of the day there are wide views towards the forest country to the east. The final part of the day is a long descent to narrow lake Sitojaure, where the birch forest re-appears.

The next day's walk is unusually short. It starts with a boat trip, continuing over a plateau-like ridge and down to the well-known farmstead of Aktse, the gateway to the Sarek. The farm mixes beautiful haymaking meadows with areas of coniferous forest, a landscape that is among the grandest on the Trail. The area is dominated by three very steep mountains, which together form the magnificent 'gateway' around the delta in Láittaure lake.

After a boat trip across the lake the Trail starts the third day, a long day that starts and ends in the forest. The Trail enters the Sarek National Park, then climbs steeply, a long climb, but one that offers new views, especially to the game-rich Rittak valley. Further on you descend into this valley, reaching real native coniferous forest with old and rugged trees. Shortly before the end of the day, the Trail leaves the Sarek Park and reaches the Pårte hut. From here you continue entirely within coniferous forest, an atmospheric landscape where you roam past a forest lake with a real wilderness feel to it, rocky shores and a backdrop of high peaks. The last lap of the fourth day is a gradual descent to the mountain village of Kvikkjokk.

9. Saltoluokta – Sitojaure

Distance: about 20km. Height gain/loss: +345m, ±40m, ±40m, -120m. Time: 6–8 hours. Strenuous.

Starting from the coniferous forest in the valley of Stora Lule river, the Trail leads up to a plateau with small undulations. You then follow a long rock face before descending to a lake in the forest.

From the jetty at Langas there is a wide, well-trodden path to the entrance of Saltoluokta fell station. The Royal Trail continues into the coniferous forest behind the buildings. After a few hundred metres, the number of pines in the forest decreases, and birch starts to dominate. The path is a wide gravel track through carpets of bilberries (*Vaccinium myrtillus*). Where the birches take over, the hard climb towards the open fell starts. The trees become increasingly more crooked and low growing, and below, through the trees, Langas lake is occasionally seen, as are the peaks on its far side.

After 1km you reach a fork in the path, where it is possible to turn west towards Pietsaure and, further on, towards Sarek. To the west, among the birches you can see the imposing precipice of Lulep Kierkau (1139m): the name means 'the mountain that looks like an upside down Sámi cradle'. This landmark is visible from almost everywhere in the area around Saltoluokta. The path is steep here, and continues to climb after the fork until you leave the birch forest behind to emerge onto dry scrub heath. To the west, cone-shaped Slugga (1279m) stands out, just over 10km away, while to the south you will also see the longish ridge of Sjäksjö (1250m), but the view is still dominated by Lulep Kierkau, which even at this angle is a towering peak, though the profile has become more rounded. Although you are in an open landscape, there is a real valley feel to the walking here.

The open landscape continues as you walk south. To the west, between Lulep Kierkau and the sharp contour of Rasek (1092m), lies the Ávtsusvágge valley. The name derives from 'brushy', but is no

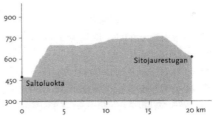

longer appropriate to today's terrain. The valley also has an alternative name, Áhusjavavágge, which means 'the valley with a deep brook which cannot be waded, only jumped across', which describes the stream in the Áhusjagårsså ravine. Áhusjavágge is a wide, spacious valley, which starts from the south and continues north-west, where the mountains hug the long and narrow Pietsaure lake.

Beyond the treeline, head towards a crest below faintly marked Käinutålke (787m). From the crest the Trail descends gently to the Ávtsusjjåhkkå river. The views are now liberatingly expansive, in sharp contrast to the view from Saltoluokta, where the walker was hemmed in by forest and steep hillsides.

Along Ávtsusjjåhkå windswept shrub heaths with sparse vegetation spread out. The heath and the river are on a geologically interesting form of terrain called a 'Pietsaure outwash plain'. It was formed during the last stage of the Ice Age from gravel deposited in layers ahead of an ice front, where the meltwater was squeezed out from the interior of the ice by strong hydrostatic pressure. This water-borne gravel formed a sediment immediately the pressure dropped, and a delta was built up in front of the ice. The running water was later dispersed in the deposited gravel heaps, the river developing a pattern of intertwining streams through its own sediment. Pietsaure is one of the largest outwash plains in the mountains, the flat surface, where the streams crossed each other leaving shallow and now dried-out furrows, is 9km long. The Ávtsusjjåhkå has also cut down through the gravel, creating a little valley of its own at the bottom of the wide depression. The Trail arrives at the edge of this valley within the valley. Willow brush grows close to the river all the way to Pietsaure lake.

As you walk, there are fine views north and south, but to the east and west they are more limited. To the west the view is obstructed by a longish and unusually smooth rock face, about 200m high, merging into a slightly rounded massif. At its southern end the massif terminates in the cone-shaped Tjirak (979m), which forms a new focus ahead. The face forms a natural boundary between the bedrock between rocks which are 400 million years old and the primary rock of the inner parts of Lapland, which is several billion years old. To the east, the obstruction is the more gradual rise to rounded peaks that continue towards Ultevis.

About halfway through the day's stage you pass a handly shelter (a *prisma*-type, with two bunks and a stove). To the west here, beyond the dramatic rock face, an undulating landscape appears: it was built up by a meltwater river during the Ice Age. From the shelter, the Trail continues along the edge of a gravelled precipice, which slopes down about 20m towards Ávtsusjåhkå. Here the river runs in a smaller valley within the valley, its banks a mass of squat willow shrubbery. Look behind here to see, to the north-west, an amusing rock nose at the top of the long rock face, standing out in sharp profile against the sky.

Next, you pass a few small tarns and descend to a point where the river must be waded. This is straightforward, followed by a sharp climb up the opposite gravelly bank. The Trail then continues parallel with a narrow, dry valley to reach a point where you can see, to the south, the Gasskajávrre and the Gåbddåjávrre lakes and their low-lying surroundings. Both lakes are basins almost cut off from the much larger mountain lake of Sitojaure. To the east, in the far distance, a shimmering blue forested country comes into view, whilke to the west some of the high peaks of the Sarek are still visible.

Further on the Trail crosses a very deep and narrow dry valley, requiring a steep descent, then ascent of about 20m. Beyond this the walk goes gently downhill. The first birches to come into view: they form a narrow belt, the walk reaching open heath surrounded by the forest. Then, to finish, the Trail rounds the forested hill of Lulep Vággevarásj and threads through shrubby forest vegetation to arrive at the overnight huts on the shore of Gasskajávrre.

The Sitojaure Huts (altitude 640m)

The huts are located beside the Vaggevaratj Sámi settlement (Sirka Sámi village). One hut is on a promontory only a few metres from the water's edge and replaces a building that burnt down in 1998. The other hut is in the forest a little further away from the lake. Altogether there are 22 beds here, and an emergency telephone.

The surroundings are low-lying: to the south, beyond the lake, the forest country has little height variation. To the west the character of the landscape is very different. Here the peaks of the Sarek rise above the treetops. You can see Dágartjåhkå (1671m) and Ruopsoktjåhkå (1971m), both with high, but rounded, summits. In front of them there is the sinister, bold precipice of Tjålebákte (1055m). From the small hut near the water's edge you can see the Sámi settlement just a few hundred metres away. A path leads to this collection of peat *kåtor* and huts set on open ground. The Sámi manage the boat traffic across Sitojaure. Walkers on their way into the Sarek cross Sitojaure to Rinim, but the Royal Trail crosses Gasskajávrre and Gåbddåjávre to Svine, a distance of about 4km.

Day excursions

1. Sitojaure is a possible starting point for excursions to Ultevis Tuottar ('tuottar' means 'an extensive flat low fell at the boundary of the forest', and 'ultevis' means 'unknown'). This is a remarkable region, about 20km by 50km in area and highly prized by reindeer herders for its excellent grazing during spring and autumn. The terrain consists of a strongly weathered and flat rock plateau with scenery highly reminiscent of Arctic tundra. In a geological sense the area lies outside the Scandinavian mountain chain, and is classed as low fell. To reach the plateau, take the path heading east from the Sámi settlement, cross the bridge over the Vuomajåkkå and climb up through the forest to the treeline. A good objective for the walk is Vuoitur (1094m), from where there is a good view of the plateau. If you continue to Point 1051m, you will have reached the heart of Ultevis Tuottar. The vegetation here is low-growing grass heath, dominated by Three-leaved Rush (*Juncus trifidus*). But from the summit the ground appears bare, the undulating, pale-coloured plains giving the plateau its unique character. Despite the enthusiasm of reindeer for the grass heath, overall the environment is poor in both flora and fauna. There are, however, Red Fox lairs in the area, and Dotterels breed here regularly. Other characteristic birds are Golden Plover, Meadow Pipit and Lapland Bunting.

From Vuoitur you also have an extensive view over the depression by Gåbddåjávrre where a patchwork of bogs, wet shrub heaths, meadows and birch forest can be seen. The area is rich in birds, with many species of waders and waterfowl.

Distance: about 20km (to Point 1051m). Height gain/loss: about ±420m. Time: 8–10 hours.

2. If you are a birdwatcher, you will have a strong reason to visit the remote back country by Gåbddåjávrre (mentioned above). Common species here are Yellow Wagtail, Wood Sandpiper, Snipe and Ruff. You might also see Jack Snipe, Dunlin, Greenshank and a number of ducks, including Northern Pintail, Teal and Wigeon.

3. Closer to the huts are the excellent viewpoints of Tjirak (979m) and Tjiraksnjurtje (1218m). Follow *Kungsleden* north up to the open fell and past the deep dry valley, which cuts into the slope below the summit. This dry valley drained water during the last stage of the Ice Age, when a lake, dammed by ice, filled the depression around Sitojaure. On the slope by the Gårsågasska ridge, on the north side of the depression, there are traces of the shoreline of this lake.

The south side of Tjirak is steep, but the peak can be easily climbed from the north. At the top there is a small saddle between two summits. The peak's name means 'the broken knife blade', reflecting this profile. The view from the lower top towards Sitojaure is formidable, but even better is the view from the higher top (Tiraksnjurtje – njurtje means 'mountain top'). Tjiraksnjurtje's summit is a stony, rather narrow ridge, which runs straight for almost a kilometre after rising from the middle of a wider ridge of grass heathland. From the top you can admire Sarek and the western part of Sitojaure, while across the lake is the 350m high, imposing cliff of Tjålebákte, with more Sarek peaks beyond. From the summit it can be seen that the lake invades the alpine world like a narrow wedge. To return to the huts, reverse the outward route. *Distance: about 16km. Height gain/loss: ±580m. Time: 5–7 hours.*

10. Sitojaure – Aktse

Distance: about 13km. Height gain/loss: +330m, -490m. Time: 3–4 hours. Normal.

The stage starts with a rather long boat trip, then takes a short walk across a low fell ridge before descending steeply through coniferous forest to the old homestead of Aktse.

The boat route to Svine is marked with buoys. Gasskajávrre (the middle lake) and Gåbddåjávrre (the broad lake) are very shallow and the surface

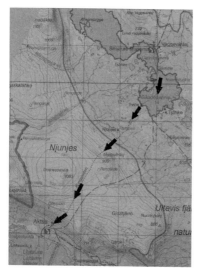

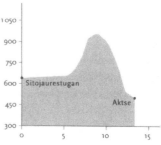

of the water can quickly become choppy, with high waves when the wind is freshening. Using the motorboat the crossing takes around 25 minutes. Those who choose to row themselves should note that to ensure that there is always a boat available for both northbound and southbound walkers they will need to complete the crossing three times. From the boat the view to the west is magnificent, the vertical cliff of Tjålebákte being a dominating feature. Below Skämmabákte (1101m) there are enormous blocks of rock formed when a large section of the peak collapsed in a landslide. Behind the Sitojaure huts the summit of Tjirak (979m) is the prominent landmark, while to the south a plateau rises beyond the low terrain close to the lakes. The plateau, called Njunjes ('an offset from a peak'), has an almost level surface and looks like a dining table. As the name indicates, it forms a promontory between Sitojaure and Láitaure lakes: it is the objective of today's stage on the Royal Trail.

At Svine there is a resting-hut near the landing stage, a useful shelter if you are waiting for the boat. The path towards Njunjes rises gently through the birch forest, crossing several cloudberry bogs on extended footbridges. Cloudberries (*Rubus chamaemorus*) are a much sought after delicacy by Scandinavians. As you walk, the view ahead is of the broad hillside that you will soon be climbing. The Trail heads towards the insignificant highest point, Mártevárás (939m), climbing through shrub heath after the treeline is reached at about 740m. Close to the top there is a small boulder field, then grassy heath as the climb steepens on the final climb. As you pause at the top, look back, towards the north to take in a view that extends far beyond Sitojaure, through the shallow Ávtsusvágge valley, to the peaks around Saltoluokta, 30–40km away. To the east the view is dominated by the rippled surface of the woodlands stretching to the horizon. Ahead, southwards, the view is more limited: you will need to cross the brow of Njunjes before it expands.

The brow is at about 960m. Once there, the first features to come into view are Tjahkkelij (1214m) and the Tjahktjajure reservoir to the south-east. The Trail now starts the descent towards Aktse, the view expanding gradually as you descend. The cliff of Skierffe soon appears, as does the colourful Láitaure lake and the vast delta in the Rapa valley. At the same time the vegetation becomes denser as you approach the treeline. Just before the forest, there is a fork in the Trail, where the path towards Skierffe heads off westward. Continue ahead on a well-trodden trail: at about 740m, you again reach birch forest. The steeply descending Trail reaches the north-east corner of the open haymaking meadow of the farmstead at Aktse and, soon, at the forest edge you reach the first buildings: these are the tourist huts.

The Aktse huts (550m)

Aktse means 'nine' and referred originally to a large split erratic boulder on the fell side above the farmstead where, according to a local legend, nine bears are said to have been killed. The clefts in the boulder are said to have been a lair used by the bears.

Today Aktse is one of the most eulogised and reproduced places in the fell world. The reason for the fame is, first and foremost, the fine edges of Skierffe, Nammásj and Tjahkkelij that surround the large Láitaure delta and form a gateway to Sarek, the high tops of which are visible. The place is also very interesting from a cultural history point of view. Several generations of settlers have lived at Aktse, surrounded by the severe mountain scenery, and isolated from the technology and comforts of larger communities. With toil and persistence the first pioneers cleared this plot of earth. The result of their work was the haymaking meadow, which has been lovingly tended through the ages. Still today it is a beautiful flower meadow, paying witness to the pioneer life. At Aktse cultivated land and wilderness have entered into a rare harmony. Originally there were just a few *kåtor* huts at Láitaure, where the reindeer migration route passed through the Rapa valley. Then at the beginning of the 1830s Pehr Amundsson Ländta and his wife Maja Larsdotter Tassa established the settler's homestead. They cleared the forest and produced a haymaking meadow of over 12 hectares, which with the sedge bogs became the foundation for their animal husbandry. They cut the grass and harvested both the meadow and the bogs. Fishing and hunting were also important elements of their natural economy. The settlement became a farmstead, which is still owned by the same family, though no one lives in Aktse throughout the year any more. Up to the 1980s the legendary brothers Wille and Sigurd Läntha were permanent residents here. Wille was responsible for the boat transportation, and Sigurd became known as a reputable hunter of large game. Today their nephew Lennart is the boatman. The Swedish Nature Conservancy Association purchased part of the homestead in 1945, and the members of the Association in Jokkmokk arrange an annual harvest weekend in July to keep the tradition alive.

On the west side of the open meadow there are now several buildings – a barn, a larger, grey two-storey house and a lower red cottage surround a small yard. Behind these buildings, nearer the edge of the forest, there are also a few sheds. The spruces in the forest form an irregular silhouette against the fells in the background, but most eye-catching is Skierffe (1179m), which looks like a giant thorn projecting dramatically above the farm and the meadow. The peak's south wall forms a free fall of 350m from the summit down to the large boulder talus, slope which continues from the base of the rock for another 350m into the Láitaure delta.

Skierffe is a crucial part of the gateway that frames the high peaks further west. In the centre of this Sarek 'gate' stands the remarkable, cubiform Nammasj (823m), and, opposite Skierffe, Tjahkkelij (1214m) is the third sentry. The latter is the most majestic mountain in the area. Tjahkkelij differs from all other Swedish mountains in being a marked plateau mountain. It has a large, almost flat and oblong summit surface, surrounded by abrupt cliffs. Along the several kilometres long north side, there is an unusually extended talus cliff, the upper part of the rock face looking like a high palisade of black rock. Between Tjahkkelij and Aktse lies Laitaure lake, though the water is partly hidden by the forest beside the meadow.

At Aktse there are three overnight huts. STF is responsible for two of these, with, altogether, 34 beds. The Swedish Nature Conservancy Association owns the third hut, built in 1959: this can also be used by walkers during the summer season. The STF warden has the key. On site there is also a telephone, and provisions can be bought. A further building is being planned. There are tent pitches around the huts. Aktse is a beautiful place, but be prepared for mosquitoes: Aktse is notorious for them.

Day excursions

1. Skierffe is the most popular destination for a day excursion in the area around Aktse. In spite of its spectacular shape, it is easy to climb from the far side. Walk back along *Kungsleden* as far as the fork in the path above the treeline. Now follow the path towards the peak, going diagonally across the hillside and passing a large glacial erratic named Aktsekallo. The view towards the delta and the high peaks in the Pårte massif to the west is magnificent. The climb is ever steeper, going up behind the shoulder of Måskotjåhkå to reach the col between Skierffe and Sliengetjåhkå (1106m). Now there is only the steep climb up Skierffe. From the summit there is a giddying sense of height and of a bottomless abyss. The drop to the delta is almost 700m, half of which is a completely vertical rock face, an astonishing height for summits of such relatively low heights above sea level.

Skierffe lies in the boundary zone between the high peaks and the forested country and as a consequence the view provides more of a bird's eye perspective than even much higher peaks can offer. To the east there is no peak reaching anything like Skierffe's height, nothing to interrupt the view across the blue-toned, rolling landscape of Lapland. Laitaure lake appears as a bright patch in the dark forest carpet in that direction. Beyond the lake you will see the wide expanse of Tjaktjajaure reservoir. The haymaking meadow at Aktse looks like a bare square in the forest. To the west the Sarek peaks appear above the Rapa valley, the summits in the Pårte and Bielloriehppe massifs helping to establish a true alpine outlook.

All this could be more than enough, but the unique feature of the view is down to the delta at the west end of Laitaure, the land and water mosaic of Råhpaädnos. The play of colours takes on a new perspective when seen from above, a palette of greyish green and turquoise-white nuances, the mix of colours due to the silt-heavy glacier water in the river meeting the dark gravel banks of the lake. The colours of the water are complemented by the lush green of the bog vegetation. By the lagoons, the small runnels and the tarns, there are often birches and dense willow thickets where you might glimpse elk or waterfowl. And if you do not suffer from vertigo, you can also admire the awesome depths of the cliff itself. To stand at the edge and look down is guaranteed to be a memorable experience!

The delta is 7km long and just over 2km wide, with an area of 10km². It is the largest in Sweden's mountain country and one of the fastest growing. About 185,000 tonnes of silt is deposited annually by the river (the equivalent of tens of thousands of lorry loads). Within a few millennia, Laitaure will be completely filled with sediment. A unique characteristic of the delta is that gravel banks are formed across the river where it reaches the lake. When the banks reach a certain size, they split the water into two arms. At present three main channels of the Råhpaädno meander through the delta. The boat for walkers heading towards Nammásj usually takes the middle channel.
Distance: about 15km. Height gain/loss: ±630m. Time: 5–7 hours.

2. Nammásj (823m) is also a rewarding day excursion. Take a boat in the morning and return to Aktse on the late afternoon boat. That way you can spend the day in the lower part of the Rapa valley and at the same time experience the fabulous boat trip through the delta. From the landing stage one can see a boulder precipice under Nammásj, and from there it is a 300m climb to the top of the mountain. The extraordinary architecture of Nammásj can be explained by the resistance in the uppermost layer of rock, which is of the same kind of primary granite as that on the top of Tjahkkelij. The best way up Nammásj is by way of the more gradually sloping and partly forested west side. The summit is a small plateau dotted with small, idyllic pools of water between flat rocks.

As a viewpoint Nammásj is excellent, with a good view of the Laitaure delta in one direction, and the lower parts of the Rapa valley in the other. The view of the delta is very different from that from Skierffe. The angle is more oblique, and all the lagoons appear closer, while behind the land/water mosaic the forest area is more dominating. To the west is the large birch forest of Ráhpavuobme: 'vuobme' means a dense continuous forest. Above the carpet of forest you can see the very high but rounded Gådoktjåhkkå (1928m). The uppermost part of Låddebákte (1537m) can be seen, with Kanalberget (1937m) further away in the background. To the south the Pårte massif is visible, with its majestic summit, Balgattjåhkkå (2002m).

The talus below the summit plateau of Nammásj has lime-rich rocks, and the flora is interesting. The peak is often referred to as a 'mountain with southern plants', the local species being more southerly than might be expected. From a botanical-geography point of view, the fact that Cut-leaved Potentilla (*Potentilla multifida*) blooms here is exciting: the plant is known to grow at about 15 locations in Scandinavia, the main distribution being in eastern Siberia. Other plants indicating great fertility and favourable climate are Norwegian Cinquefoil (*Potentilla norvegica*), Herb Paris (*Paris quadrifolia*), Baneberry (*Actaea spicata*), Northern Moonwort (*Botrychium boreale*), Alpine Woodsia (*Woodsia alpine*), Snowy Cinquefoil (*Potentilla nivea*), Lapland

Rhododendron (*Rhododendron lapponicum*), Northern Primrose (*Primula scandinavica*) and Arctic Bellflower (*Campanula uniflora*). *Distance: about 4km. Height gain/loss: ±320m. Time: all day.*

3. Tjahkkelij is less frequently climbed than the other summits around the Laitaure delta, in part because an excursion requires two boats. Please pay great attention to the boat timetable if you are planning a day trip.

But although Tjahkkelij is difficult to reach, it is, in my opinion, just as rewarding and interesting as the other two. From the landing stage on the south shore of Laitaure climb the eastern side of the peak. High up there is a vertical cleft, a seemingly impassable obstacle when first viewed from above the treeline. But it is actually easy to negotiate, and provides an interesting cross-section of the geology of the area. The lower part of the cliff is gneiss, while higher up there is a series of layered schists and sandstones, constructed from ocean sediments rich in lime. The flora is therefore prolific, the southern slopes of Tjahkkelij being another 'southern plant mountain'. Some of the more interesting plants are Holly Fern (*Polystichum lonchitis*), Norwegian Milkwort (*Astragalus norvegicus*), Lapland Rhododendron, Slender Gentian (*Gentianella tenella*), Rock Speedwell (*Veronica fruticans*), Common Kidney-Vetch (*Anthyllis vulneraria*), Pink Lousewort (*Pedicularis rosea*), Arctic Bellflower, Alpine Arnica (*Arnica alpina*) and Northern Catchfly (*Silene uralensis*).

Higher up in the gully you will see mylonite, a fine-grained, deformed rock created by faulting. In this case the base rock was syenite, an acidic volcanic granite with slight violet hue. Above the gully, the upperpart of the peak is of coarse-grained granite, the summit being a large rolling plateau of granite slabs.

The view from Tjahkkelij has many similarities with that from Skierffe, but one advantage is that you will have the light behind you at noon. Another advantage is that the view over Rapadalen is more extensive, especially from the western part of the summit plateau. The word *rapa* probably derives from the Ráhpaädno river, and means 'to travel fast': the name Rapadalen is a hybrid Sámi-Swedish word. The valley lies between the high Sarek peaks and through it Ráhpaädno meanders like a bright ribbon through the forest. Olgásj (1918m) and Miehtsee Skoarkki (1828m) are the most prominent peaks on each side of the valley. The panorama as a whole gives an overwhelming impression of an untouched mountain landscape. Some peaks in the far distance, for instance Tarrekaise (1828m) can also be seen to the west, as can the carpet of the Ráhpavuobme forest.

It is possible to pitch a tent on the plateau: water can be obtained from a small tarn at the western edge.

Distance: about 12km (to Point 1162m). Height gain/loss: ±670m. Time: 6–8 hours.

4. The Laitaure delta is a perfect location for birdwatching, many waders and waterfowl being attracted to the tied off lagoons where the temperature of the water and the salt content rise, favouring biological production. The delta has been named a wetland of international importance because of the birdlife and is thus on the CW (Convention of Wetlands) list. Species that breed regularly include Whooper Swan, Teal, Wigeon, Northern Pintail, Tufted Duck, Wood Sandpiper, Greenshank and Red-necked Phalarope. A southern species that is seen here is the Sedge Warbler. Many birds of prey and some owls also pass through this area, among them White-tailed Eagle, Golden Eagle, Osprey, Gyrfalcon, Kestrel, Short-eared Owl and Hawk Owl. Around the delta there are varied habitats for a large number of birds; 85 species have been recorded around Aktse during a single summer season. But the delta is difficult to get to, and visitors are advised not to make their own way there as this risks disturbing the wildlife. You are also not allowed to use boats to explore the delta. Therefore, if you wish to watch for birds, you should bring a telescope with high magnification and watch from the surrounding hillsides.

5. An old Sámi sacrificial place below Skierffe is also a rewarding destination. From the west corner of the haymaking meadow at Aktse,

there is a poorly trodden path heading west. Take this: where it peters out you will have to make your own way and walking in the dense forest is hard going. Aim for the boulder precipice below Skierffe to reach Sáivva lake (the name, in Lule Sámi dialect, indicates that the lake is holy, though in other dialects it means a lake without an outlet). Beside the lake there is an old, and at one time very important, cave. The cave is close to the water, and is formed from huge blocks of stone piled up to form a small cavity. Here the Sámi once prayed to their gods and made sacrifices. It is perhaps understandable that the place was seen as special: the scenery is overwhelming, with Skierffe towering up into the sky, while the vast boulders are impressive. However, they are also quite hazardous, as new landslips can be easily set off, so take great care.

Distance: about 10km. Height gain/loss: none. Time: 2–4 hours.

11. Aktse – The Pårte Huts

Distance: about 20km. Height gain/loss: +325m, ±40m, ±20m, -345m. Time: 8–10 hours. Strenuous.

On this stage you will first walk through coniferous forest, then across open fell and down into the coniferous forest again. The walk is long and strenuous, but also interesting in its variety: the forest is original coniferous, and you pass through a corner of the Sarek National Park.

To start follow the path from the huts past the hut belonging to the Nature Conservancy Association and across extended footbridges to reach the edge of the forest. Go down through the spruce forest on further footbridges, to reach the jetty at Laitaure. From the shore the whole of the Sarek gateway is seen to its best advantage, the mountains forming an impressive framework for the colourful water in the foreground. The inner mountain world of Sarek can be seen: look out for the Bielloriehppe massif, characterised by dragon-like ridges.

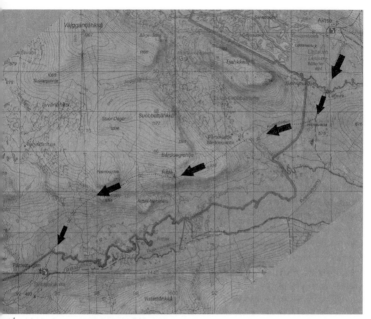

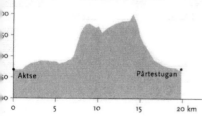

If you wish to row across the lake, there are rowing boats, which can be borrowed. The rowing route is marked with buoys. With the fast, open motor boat the crossing takes about 15 minutes. Either way, the mountains, seen from Laitaure, are powerful natural scenery, even more imposing from this perspective than from Aktse. Skierffe's precipice appears to have increased in height, the cubiform shape of Nammásj has become even more symmetric, and the long north wall gives Tjahkkelij the appearance of being an impregnable fort. The boat passes one of the small islets in the lake and reaches the opposite landing stage, set in a protected little cove. Above the shore there is a *prisma* shelter with bunks and a stove. Across the lake you can see the extended slope of Njunje curving down towards the coniferous forest around Aktse: you crossed that area on your journey here. The Sarek gateway has now disappeared behind the forest, only Tjahkkelij remaining impressive. From here you can see that the short east side of the mountain looks similar to that of Nammásj.

The Trail starts with an easy stretch on relatively level ground as far as the bridge across Suobbatjåhkå. The forest here is both spruce and mountain birch. Halfway to the bridge you enter the Sarek National Park. Beyond the bridge there are fewer spruce, and they end altogether when you climb steeply up through the birch forest belt to reach the open fell below Bårddegiehtje (*giehtje* means 'end'). Now the view northwards expands, including the extensive valley between Tjahkkelij and Suobbattjåhkkå (1177m). *Suobbat* means 'a snow bridge across a river or a cleft' and probably derives from the Suobbatjåhkå brook. The valley can be regarded as an offshoot of the Rapa valley and is a favourite haunt of elk. In its extension northwards, the Skårki massif becomes visible, and you will also see the light-coloured surface of the Alep Vássjájiegna glacier and the characteristic flattened summit of Miehtsse Skoarkki (1842m).

The trek along the fell continues to provide extensive views. Below, to the south, is the Rittak valley and Rittak lake. The lake still has its natural shoreline despite being an inlet to the vast Tjaktjajaure reservoir: you can also see most of this giant artificial lake. The water level varies by up to 34.5m, and when the level is low, the shore areas look desolate. By contrast, when the level is high, the reservoir can, like all great expanses of water, look attractive, as if it were a natural feature of the landscape. The damming of Tjaktjajaure was one of the largest ever acts of interference in the Swedish landscape, 7200 hectares of ground having been flooded. But despite the vast size of the lake, the

Ritta valley is still rich in game. It is used by many animals as a link between the Rapa valley and Njoatjosvágge. Bear, Lynx and Wolverine often stay in the valley, while Golden Eagle and White-tailed Eagle regularly fly over. On the west shore of Rittak there are large wetlands, a brilliant green patch in the dull coniferous forest. On the south side of the valley the landscape takes on a greyish hue from the low Kabla fell (the name probably indicating that it represents the end of the high peak area). At its highest Kabla rises to only 1188m, forming a plateau-like island in the forest.

After a few kilometres the Trail descends towards the treeline. By the first birches you will find the Rittak shelter and a latrine. Beyond, you leave the forest, going slightly up and across the hillside on easy ground. Soon, ahead, you will see the pass between Favnoajvve (1117m) and Huornnásj (884m). Favnoajvve has a high and very steep southern side, the Trail passing between this and the treeline as it climbs to the pass, where new, and overwhelming, views appear, including the western parts of the Rittak valley, forming an extensive depression between the Gállakvárre (1125m), Nuortab Sjábttjakvárre (832m) and Kabla. The whole depression is covered by a dense, untouched carpet of forest and, among the conifers, the shining surface of the Sjabtjakaure lake becomes visible. The lake is the destination for this stage. Distant peaks can also be seen – Pårtetjåkkå (2005m) and the characteristic profile of Kaskåive (1322m) by the Tarra valley. Far away in the distance you may also see the rounded peaks to the west of Kvikkjokk. If weather conditions are right, the pass also has a strong echo, sounds being hurled back and forth between the hillsides.

The Trail descends steeply from the pass to reach a dense birch forest rich in plants. Further on the path becomes stony and heavy going, not least because it is the last part of a long day's walk. In the forest there are some very tall plants, including Alpine Sow-Thistle (*Cicerbita alpina*) and Northern Wolfsbane (*Aconitum septentrionale*). As you descend there are more spruce, and after crossing the bridge over

Kallatjåkkå, pine becomes more and more common. Here the Trail is passing through pristine coniferous forest, with dead trees and old decomposing tree trunks on the ground, the old trees providing a counterbalance to the open fell country and making the stage feel varied, with different landscapes offering different aesthetic values. Such variety is the classic wilderness of the 'land in the north', an ancient large forest surrounded by high mountains.

The Trail now passes through several small boggy glades and follows some occasional ridge lines. At the bridge you leave the Sarek National Park: now complete the last couple of kilometres to reach the Pårte huts.

The Pårte huts (500m)

The two huts are situated on a headland thrust into the beautiful Sjabtjakjaure lake (*sjabtjak* means 'schist' and refers to the bedrock around the lake). On the far side of the lake, Tuottartjåkkå reaches above the trees: thanks to the peak, the feeling of being in the mountains is preserved because the view would otherwise be very limited, the conifers growing right up to the shores of the clear lake. However, the forest radiates a romantic atmosphere, something that can only be found deep within a pathless wilderness. The first hut here was built in 1890, but burnt down the same year. The older of the two buildings now on the site was constructed in the 1960s and has 20 beds and an emergency telephone. There is also a newer building with sleeping space for six persons and a warden's room. Camping is possible nearby.

Day excursions

1. The Pårte huts can be used a starting point for excursions into the local, primeval forest. In the Rittak valley you will find one of the most unspoiled forests in Sweden, so please make the most of the opportunity to become familiar with this unique landscape. The Sarek National Park has provided protection for these trees since 1909. If you retrace *Kungsleden* to the bridge over Sjabtjakjåkkåtj and then head off

down towards the bogs by Rittak lake you will likely see typical woodland birds including Siberian Jay and Siberian Tit. In the Rittak valley there is also a large number of Capercaillie. Many of the pines show traces of forest fire – deep cuts on the lower parts of the trunks where the bark has thickened into large calluses, the cuts having been caused by fire, a natural hazard. During the 1980s, a forest fire was started by lightning on the slope below Huornatj causing a dilemma for the National Park management – should they fight the fire or allow it to burn? The fire threatened a large area, including the Pårte huts. Both ground-based fire fighters and a helicopter had to be employed to bring the fire under control, and they restricted destruction to just 2–3 hectares. The area of the fire, desolate and studded with charred tree skeletons, is worth visiting.

2. In the vicinity of the huts there are a few viewpoints of interest. You can make your own way through the forest to Nuortap Sjábttjakvárre (832m), while a longer excursion takes in Point 1135m north of Stuortjåhkkå. This peak is situated south of the Pårte huts and you will need to ford Rittakjjåhko: this is straightforward close to the outflow from Sjabtjakjaure. Beyond the ford, walk south, then follow a brook uphill.
Distance: about 10km. Height gain/loss: ±650m. Time: 5–7 hours.

3. Higher summits of interest, although they are further away, are Gállakvárre (1125m) and Faunåive (1117m). The latter peak is easier to reach: follow *Kungsleden* up through the forest to the pass by Huornatj and from there climb to the summit along the west and north slopes. The view towards Sarek is tremendous, taking in the high summits of Bielloriehppe.
Distance: about 14km. Height gain/loss: ±620m. Time: 5–7 hours.

12.   The Pårte Huts – Kvikkjokk

**Distance: about 16km. Height gain/loss: +60m, -80m, +20m, -190m.
Time: 5–6 hours. Normal.**

*This whole stage is within the forest, a powerful experience. When there are
views, they are of the high peaks in Tarrrekaise.*

The Trail between the Sjabtjakjaure and Stuor Tata lakes is, in parts,
stony as it leads you through an ancient forest, the dark, primeval trees
brightened only by the delightful, babbling brook of Tjåltajåkkå, which
is crossed by a bridge. Further on, by the Jåkkåkaska Sámi village, a
reindeer fence is crossed, just before the walker reaches Stuor Tata lake.
The lake's name apparently derives from a misunderstanding, a
cartographer asking a Sámi man for its name, and getting the answer
'tata?' – 'this one?'. The lake is relatively large and breaks up the closed
world of the forest. Far away on the other side you will Vallespiken
(1385m), the highest point behind the ridges of the forest. The top
part of the much lower Karvek (774m) is also visible. The walk along
the lake shore is very attractive, the few islets enhancing the beauty of
the lake. As you proceed, the sharp pinnacle on Vuokspakte (1065m)
comes into view.

After about a kilometre of very scenic walking you enter the forest
again. The path is initially monotonous, in part because there is no
original forest left, the local inhabitants having felled the trees regularly.
The Trail climbs slightly, offering occasional glimpses of Kabla, to the
east. Then, after about a kilometre you begin a gentle descent, bogs
adding variety to the landscape. By the bridge across Njakajåkkå there
is an area of fine scenery, an open bog against a background of forest
and a distant backdrop of mountain ridges above the trees. There are
some popular resting places here, and you may meet walkers on day
excursions from Kvikkjokk. Beyond the bridge, the Trail climbs a little,

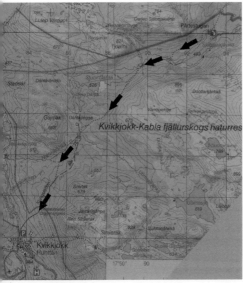

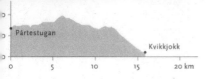

then begins a descent towards the village. The forest is dense now, though in places there is a rich lower growth of flora.

As you approach Kvikkjokk there are a few sections of sharper gradient, and the sounds of civilisation intrude – dogs barking, cars starting – a reminder of the vulnerability of the mountain landscape. The Trail crosses a vast clearing, only a small strip of tall forest remaining, just 5–10m wide and a few hundred metres long, saved to spare walkers a view of the devastation. The consequence was that the exposed trees were uprooted during a storm at the end of the 1980s, many trees falling across the Trail. The fallen trees were left for a long time, walkers making many paths around them. But now order has been restored, with birch saplings starting to sprout in the clearing, though as yet the new growth cannot be compared with the wonderful forest that you have just left behind. Soon after the clearing a tractor track takes the Royal Trail to the Kvikkjokk fell station, set next to the roaring rapids of Kamjåkkå.

KVIKKJOKK –

Distance: about 96km. Height gain/loss:

This is the least popular stretch of the Royal Trail, one explanation, perhaps, being the absence of huts, another the long boat crossings required, which might act as deterrent. There is also a persistent rumour that the landscape is not as interesting as the sections to the north and further south.

I totally disagree with that suggestion. Indeed, I think that this section of the Trail is underestimated and should attract many more walkers. Apart from the need to carry a tent and the fact that the path is not always very clear, it is no more difficult to walk, and the boat crossings can be easily arranged when you arrive at the lakes. And despite its reputation, the landscape is both different from the other walk sections, and magnificent. The expansive landscapes you will cross contribute to the great variety that is one of the strengths of the Trail. Here you are in the transition zone between two landscape types. To the east is the vast inland of Lapland, with its shimmering blue heights, while to the west the high peaks form a precipitous wall. For long stretches you are completely enclosed in the bosom of the forest, yet at other times you will be walking across flat fell ridges that offer more extensive views than any other points along the Trail.

The Trail starts with a boat crossing of Sakkat lake to Mallenjarka after which you will spend the day in a timeless

– JÄKKVIK

+2230m, -1970m. Time: 7 days.

wilderness. The Trail passes through a corner of the Pärlälven Nature Reserve, an area of old, untouched coniferous forest surrounded by high mountains. Here the Trail ascends steeply in three steps to reach a flat upland clad by an amazingly beautiful birch forest. At the southern edge of this area is the Tsielekjåhkå river where you will find a small *prisma* hut. From here the prospects are vast, as you continue over a fell ridge and down into the wide valley of the Pite river, where you will need to find somewhere to pitch your tent in the coniferous forest.

On the next stage the Trail crosses the torrents of the Pite river on bridges, and then climbs over yet another fell ridge, Barturtte, which projects out from the high fells towards the distant forest in the east, like an endless tongue. Up here the views are far-reaching, and I recommend that you camp on the south side of the ridge. On the next stage the Trail descends into a large area of birch forest, the path sweeping past several cosy small lakes to reach Vuonatjviken, an old settlement, now with huts and a restaurant for walkers. The last stage before Jäkkvik starts with a boat lift across Riebnes and a walk over the next low fell ridge, Tjidjakvalle, followed by a long boat crossing over Hornavan from Saudal to Jäkkvik.

13. Kvikkjokk – Tsielekjåhkå

Distance: about 15km. Height gain/loss: +260m, -20m, +220m, -180m. Time: 5–7 hours. Normal.

South of Kvikkjokk the Trail spends time in coniferous forest, part of the Pärlälven primeval fell forest nature reserve. Higher up, the terrain turns into a level plateau with the most attractive birch forests you could imagine.

The path starts at Mallenjarka, a beautiful homestead on a promontory in Sakkat lake. To reach the homestead, you will need to take the boat from Kvikkjokk: you need to book your trip with the boatmen – ask for details at the fell station. If you arrive at Mallenjarka from the south, you will have to book the boat to Kvikkjokk in advance: the safest thing is to carry a mobile telephone.

Around midsummer there is a fascinating display of flowers in the meadow around the Mallenjarka homestead, while beyond the forest to the west, high above the silhouette of sprawling spruces, the rocks of solitary Nammás (657m) gleam in the distance. From this angle, the upper part of the mountain looks like a skullcap. Through the birches on the shore of Sakkat, and across the wide expanse of water, Bårddetjåhkkå (2005m) in Sarek can be seen, rising majestically like a long and unbroken mountain chain. Below, and much nearer, are houses of Kvikkjokk set within the sloping forest. Further towards the east, the view is spoilt by an unsightly clearing.

Mallenjarka was established by Jacob Daniel Mannberg. His father came to Kvikkjokk at the beginning of the 19th century, and in 1856 he built the first houses. The village was inhabited by the same family until the middle 1960s, but now the houses are for holiday use only. The name Mallenjarka means 'blood peninsula' and derives from the swarms of mosquitoes Mannberg encountered. The name has stuck, despite some owners wanting to change it to the more sympathetic 'mill point'. The Royal Trail crosses the little meadow and heads into the forest in the direction of Nammásj. You follow the edge of a bog

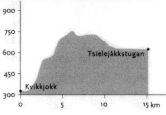

on relatively level terrain through the pines. After about a kilometre, spruce becomes the dominant tree species: here you start the steep climb of the first 'step' of the stage, the Trail becoming stonier and the walking laborious. But soon you will hear a noisy brook near the path, and higher up, there is a small waterfall where the Trail crosses a steep brook ravine, a good place to rest and quench your thirst. Through the gaps in the spruce here you can make out, to the north, Unna Skoarkki (1812m) by the Rapa valley in Sarek, almost 50km away.

The Trail climbs straight up, but then, after another kilometre, climbs diagonally before rounding a clearly defined, forested hill where you look down towards a peaceful little tarn. Between the trees, the view now opens up westwards, extending over a fine wilderness landscape. The topography is hilly, and beyond the undulating forest curtains in the foreground there are high peaks. To the north-west, between the slender spruces, the scarred precipices of Kaskåive (1322m) can be seen, while more towards the west, and even further away, is the high summit of Staike (1794m). The Trail now goes briefly downhill to reach a long, narrow bog where the view to the west is even more open.

Beyond the bog, you begin the climb of the 'second step', heading up through spruce forest. The Trail crosses a reindeer fence to reach a much more open birch forest where the terrain levels out. Now the view northwards, behind you, is more extensive and inspiring. Beyond the rolling forest hills in the foreground you will be able to see several of the southern Sarek summits, including Ryggåsberget (1946m), Balgattjåhkkå (2002m), Bårddetjåhkkå (2005m) and Skáidejågås (1933m). To the north-east, plateau-like low fell massifs such as Kabla (1188m) and Kassavare (957m) rise above the rolling forest sea.

The Trail now continues through the birch forest, passing a few open bogs before climbing the 'third step'. You climb over a forested mountain ridge and, beyond the high point, descend a short, but very steep slope. Before descending be sure to take in the view over a fascinating upland, with open birch forest growing on almost level ground. This unusual type of landscape spreads eastwards, where a faintly marked hill, Lástakvárddo (799m), hides Peurare lake. To the south, this calm landscape extends just over 5km towards Sjiellabuollda: that is the next objective of the Trail. Finally, to the west the upland becomes spacious and is framed by the massifs situated to the north and south of the Tarra valley, an area that is home to Bear and Wolverine.

You descend to enter a park-like forest area, unique for the fells. The view through the slender and low birches is very good, and the level terrain, together with the dry ground and the grass-dominated undergrowth makes the area look like a savanna forest. Beautiful glades open up in several places, and in these you will see some solitary junipers. Decayed tree-trunks can be see here and there. The walking is easy here, with no appreciable height gains or losses, until you reach a slight downhill slope at the end of the 'park'. After traversing this unusual forest landscape, the free-standing and striking summit of Vuoka (1248m) appears through the trees. The more bulky Tarrekaise (1828m) can also be seen, both mountains become even more prominent when seen from the bogs that lead towards Tsielekjåhkå (the name means 'barking brook'). The rushing sound of the river will soon be heard, but the water remains hidden for a long time behind forested ridges. About a kilometre before the stream you pass a natural spring, which is handy for filling water bottles. The Trail then circles a ridge to reach a suspension bridge over the river and the little *prisma* hut, which is the destination for this stage.

The Tsielekjåhkå hut (630m)

The STF-owned hut has two bunks and a stove, but firewood is not supplied. The hut stands on a bare gravel terrace, about 5m high, above the gushing river. From the site there are fine views east and west, but to the north the view is obscured by the forested upland. To the south there is a high fell slope. Clumps of birch forest of varying sizes dominate the local surroundings, but to the east, downstream, the forest is more continuous. In that direction the landscape appears as a shallow valley, which guides the eye to steep Pavvaltjåhkkå (900m) by Peurare lake, 15km away (though the lake itself is not visible).

To the west, upstream, the landscape does not have the same valley appearance. Here, an uneven upland spreads out, bordered to the south by the wide Sjellabuollda ('sacrifice slope'), the highest point of which, at 1551m, forms a conical profile above the slope. The most sensational mountain in the area is Vuoka (1248m), to the north-west, which can be recognised by its boat-shaped silhouette. Seen from the hut, the summit rises beautifully over Tsielekjåhkå. As you look due south, the fell slope curves in like a valley and merges into a narrow ravine, Suongergårsså, where the Royal Trail will continue tomorrow.

Day excursions

1. A long, arduous but rewarding day excursion visits the fell homestead of Skaite, situated by the Tsielekjåhkå near its outflow into Peurare lake. Follow the river eastwards from the hut, and after about 4km you will reach a small smokehouse by a reindeer fence crossing the river. From there a path leads down to Skaite. The settlement was established by Skaite-Janne and his wife Maria who came here in 1910. They first lived in a peat *kåta*, but later built a house for which they did not have permission. The boundaries between Crown land and private

land were drawn up at the time of distribution of lands in 1918. At that time the settlement was classed as a fell dwelling, but that it stood on Crown land. The building therefore had to be leased from the State and certain rules were set on the owners. The homestead was occupied until 1964 and then stood empty for ten years: it was then converted into a private holiday home.

The building stands in a cleared and inviting glade deep within the dark spruce forest. Several small sheds are scattered around the meadow, which is approximately square and is full of flowering plants in mid-summer. The name Skaite means 'the land between two merging rivers' and refers to the homestead's position between Tsielejåhkå and Bárkájåhkå. There is an emergency telephone here. Behind the dwelling house, looking due south, one can see the precipitous rocks of Bednakbákte and the boulder-strewn talus at its base. The fertile Peurare delta lies about a kilometre further east: bog harvests used to be carried out there. The delta is silting unusually slowly, far more slowly than, for instance, the Kvikkjokk delta, the reason being that Tsielekjåhkå does not carry any glacier silt, so that only relatively small amounts of sand and gravel are deposited.

From the summit of Bednakbákte there is a grand view of the beautiful ante-fell landscape. To reach it, ford the usually slow-running Bárkájåhkå. From the summit there is a fine view, both of the delta and the western part of the Pärlälven Nature Reserve. However, the view is dominated by the endless coniferous forest carpet, the meadow at Skaite shining out as a bright patch. In the background there is a hint of the wild summits of Sarek: all in all, the panorama captures the essence of the Lapland wilderness.

Distance: about 20km. Height gain/loss: ±170–250m. Time: 8–10 hours.

2. From Tsielekjåhkå you can easily climb Goabddátjåhkkå (1462 m – the name means 'the mountain of the troll drum'). This summit offers an interesting view of the local high peaks. To start, follow *Kungsleden* south for a couple of kilometres to the treeline, and then continue straight up along the fall line on the Sjpietjam ridge. In the

past, *Kungsleden* followed this line, and the old path can still occasionally be traced, but the Trail has now been re-routed. Higher up the ground levels out, becoming a large, airy plateau with open views in all directions except towards the west, where Goabddåtjåhkkå rises. The old Trail crossed the peak, which despite its height has a level summit, the work of millennia of erosion. The plateau has a diameter of a couple of kilometres and is sparsely covered with grass between the boulders. Towards the east the view is limitless. You can see the profile of Dundret 130km away, while to the far south is the Barturtte ridge, which you will cross on the Trail. To the north you can see the whole of the large upland around Tsielekjåhkå, with the Sarek peaks providing a backdrop.

Continue across the plateau then climb through steep, bouldery terrain to reach the true summit of Goabddátjåhkkå, which may still have snow patches in midsummer. The summit is actually a 5km, rather narrow ridge, reaching 1551m at the north-western end. From the summit cairn the view towards the west is dominated by high peaks, while right below your feet there is a deep, narrow U-shaped valley, Fálesvágge, which cuts between Goabddátjåhkkå and the more rounded Ráskka (1456m). All the tops in this massif have convex summits, and although the landscape is very hilly, you will not see any sharp ridgelines. However, Riehpentjåhkkå (1464m) has several vertical precipices dropping down towards Fálesvágge.

By following the ridge from Goabddátjåhkkå southwards (at the same time dropping a couple of hundred metres in altitude), you can reach Goabddábakte (1266m), where the massif ends abruptly with a cliff. From this summit you have a good view of the area to the south where the Trail continues. You will also see the extensive valley by the Parka Sámi settlement (Tuorpon Sámi village). Further to the south-west, the topography is dominated by the wide valley of the Pite river, where the large Tjieggelvas lake can be seen. From Goabddábakte you can drop down to the Trail and follow it back to the hut.

Distance: about 19km. Height gain/loss: ±830m (to Goabddátjåhkkå).
Time: 8–10 hours.

14. Tsielekjåhkå – Gistojávrátj

Distance: about 18km. Height gain/loss: +320m, -360m, ±40m. Time: 7–9 hours. Strenuous.

On this stage you will reach a plateau with expansive views, then make a long descent to the coniferous forest in the Pite river valley.

Immediately beyond the hut, the Trail winds between scattered clumps of fell birch, the forest being dispersed on the slope. The ground is boggy in places, but above the treeline, drier bilberry (*Vaccinium myrtillus*) heath dominates.

The view backwards expands as you climb, with even more peaks becoming visible. Peurare lake is also added to the panorama. The extensive uplands are characterised by modest ridges and a mosaic of bog and patchy forest, while in the far distance, the high peaks form a decorative backdrop. Vuoka (1248m) has an exceptionally beautiful shape from this side. To the north of it, several Sarek peaks come into view, including rounded Tarrekaise (1828m) and Bårdetjåhkkå (1908m), and, like a fascinating mirage through a Y-shaped gap between the closer mountains Ridhátjåhkkå (1944m), in the centre of Sarek, 55km away, can be seen.

After a modest ascent you will reach the 2km ravine valley of Suongergårsså. The ravine is about a kilometre wide at first, but narrows, wedge-like, into a tight and rather steep ravine. Here the Trail crosses a discreet, but geologically significant, boundary as you leave middle nappe bedrock, which spans the area around Kvikkjokk, and reach the upper, so-called Seve-Köli nappe, which forms the large high fell area to the west.

As you follow the new Trail, marked out at the end of the 1980s, in Suongerkårså the hillsides shield far views, but there are fine, closer views of the plant life of the valley floor. As you now climb the steep and boulder-strewn slope at the far end of the valley, the vast view behind returns: with the help of binoculars you will be able to make

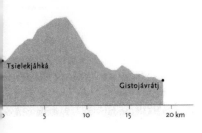

out high Sarek summits such as Ruopsotjåhkkå (1914m) in Äpar, Unna Skoarkki (1802m) and Gådotjåhkkå (1928m).

From the ravine the Trail ascends to a relatively large high plateau, which allows views towards the south and east, across characterless, but still significant, low fell massifs and forest ridges. Beyond Spietjamválle (1020m, the name means 'the east end of a fell which juts out towards the east') you can just make out the deep valley where Parkajaure lake lies. The landmark ahead is Goabddábakte (1266m), a substantial rock face with an impressive 300m drop.

The going improves as you soak up the view, the grass heath being easy to walk on. Continue towards the north slope of the plateau and then go on a slight diagonal towards Goabddábakte, approaching a long and eye-catching ridge that follows the southern edge of the plateau. The ridge has been asymmetrically formed, and is about 8m high on the side that faces you, but more than double that on the other side. Soerggajågåsj brook cuts right through the ridge in one

117

place, and through this gap the Parka Sámi settlement can be seen far down in the surprisingly deep valley to the south. Researchers used to think that the ridge was gravel brought here by meltwater from the last Ice Age, but recent investigations indicate that it is a very old moraine ridge, which was not ploughed away by the last Ice Age as the ice had frozen solidly to the ground here.

The stream is easily forded where it runs to the east of Goabddábakte. Beyond you will find yourself next to the mountain's black amphibolite cliff, at the foot of which is a 10–20m scree slope, many of the bigger boulders covered with Map Lichen (*Rhizocarpon geographicum*), which gives them a pale yellow hue against the black background. Where the Trail passes nearest to the mountain, there is a good echo, adding to the drama of the rocks pointing straight up into the sky. In places, slip gullies have split the massive rock face, the eastern part standing up almost like an independent rock pillar. The views are also good here: to the south you will see the valley of the Pite river as well as the low peaks of Áksega (1271m) and Barturtte (1003m), attached to form a long, unbroken backwash to the wide river valley. The large Tjieggelvas lake can be recognised by its characteristic hourglass shape.

From the cliff, the Trail continues down a stony slope called Sierggabuollda ('the willow hill'), and after 3km you regain birch forest, though the forest here is diffuse. The Trail now runs parallel to Fálesjåhkå, which is hidden in a cleft. In the cleft there is a bridge for those who wish to walk westwards: the Trail does not go that way, continuing down a set of three natural steps of gravel. These terraces are an Ice Age remnant, built up by meltwater that deposited gravel against an ice edge in the bottom of the valley. Between each terrace there is a small drop.

Beyond the steps, the Trail turns away from Fálesjåhkå and continues through the birch forest towards Ruovvdejávre lake. You will pass bogs, where there is a good chance of spotting waders such as Greenshank and Curlew, before the Trail climbs to the forested height of Alep Saddermtjåhkkå (670m). After just over 1 kilometre you will reach a small moraine ridge, which offers a fine view towards the west where Fálesjávre in the Pite river lake chain appears, surrounded by forest-covered hills. To the north are the tall summits of Ráskka (1456m) and Goabddábakte (1266m). More and more pines now grow around the trail: the forest here is a favourite haunt of Capercaillie, their droppings often being seen on the path. Continue down the slopes of Alep Saddermtjåhkkå on a rather stony path, with a view to Árdná (1035m), 10km away, south of the Pite river, its summit looking rather like a swelling.

You can camp by Gistojávrátj lake, close to the Trail here, a pleasant spot with a great atmosphere, the lake being surrounded by forest on rocky ground, and some bogs. Behind the tree curtain on the north shore, the upper parts of the Ráskka and Goabddábakte reappear.

Day excursions
1. The village of Västerfjäll is an interesting destination from the campsite. It is best reached by following the old *Kungsleden* trail, which threads through an old pine forest with rugged trees, boulders and rocky ground. Many pines have been cut down here, halting the natural spread of the trees. The village is located on an inlet of the north shore of Tjieggelvas, well protected from the prevailing west and north-west winds. The cleared open ground is relatively large (about 15 hectares), the buildings, houses and barns, being spread across it. In the inlet there are a few small islets, where potatoes (again the so-called 'almond' potato) used to be grown on relatively frost-free soil. To the south, Tjieggelvas spreads out, surrounded by tranquil forest heights. To the west, Árdná (1035m – name means 'eagle') has a surf-like appearance. The first settlement here was built by the Sámi in 1863. When the distribution of land occurred in the 1880s, the homestead was already well established, and the farms were regarded as freehold farms. The village land was therefore demarcated as a large private enclave (covering 4600 hectares) deep within the vast State-owned

lands (today called Crown Surplus Lands). At one time, 50–60 people (adults and children) lived here, but the village was very remote and difficult to access. Barley and potatoes were grown, with goats and pigs, horses and cows being reared. The villagers also hunted and fished. After the 1939–45 War there was some forestry on village land, the timber being floated on lake and river to a sawmill at Norra Bergnäs. There was also regular boat traffic to the south end of Tjieggelva. But the old way of life was slowly receding, despite the fact that the villagers built their own chapel as late as the 1970s. In 1985 the last permanent residents left, the village becoming a summer paradise for a new generation of farmers and their families who make it a lively place, especially during the church festivals. At such times it may be possible to find accommodation.

15. Gistojávrátj – Båråktjåhkkå

Distance: about 20km (to Gásaklahko). Height gain/loss: -60m, +570m, -100m. Time: 7–9 hours. Strenuous.

The Royal Trail continues down to the majestic Pite river, which is crossed by two bridges. After a strenuous climb you reach level fell heaths and then walk across a wide and flat fell ridge with boundless views. Camping is possible on the slope on the opposite side, with all the views in front of you.

After walking about 2km from Gistojávrátj, the roar of the Pite river can be heard. When the river is reached, you will see a wide river basin, with a few huts on the north bank. The Trail sweeps along beside the river, which has a long stretch of rapids between Fálesjávre and Tjieggelvas lakes. Low rocks line the river banks, waves constantly lapping around, pine trees overlooking the scene from the rocky ground above. The combination looks rather like an archipelago forest.

When you reach a bridge there is a fine view of the majestic waterfall in Salvojåhkå, in the distance, to the west. Closer to you, the white foam

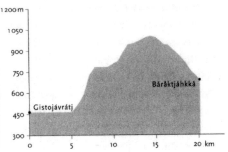

torrents of the river are awe-inspiring. Far behind, the top of Goabddábakte, with its black cliff, appears: the peak is an ever-present high landmark in this area. The river now emerges into a curved inlet of Tjieggalvas, while above the lake rises Árdná, the most prominent profile looking south.

Cross the Pite river on two suspension bridges that meet on a rocky islet. Once across, the Trail follows the shore of Tjieggelvas past a boathouse. This stretch of the Trail was re-routed at the end of the 1980s at the same time as the bridges were constructed. After about 1 kilometre you reach the power line which provides power to Västerfjäll. Here, an indistinct track goes along the narrow cleared 'street' of the power line, following a route through brushy, marshy country. The 'street' is followed for a couple of kilometres, then the Trail turns through a plant-rich forest to reach Tjålmukjavratja lake, where the forest thins out. The path is poorly cleared here, but it is easy enough to follow, an indistinct path goes straight towards the northernmost lake. Blue-headed Wagtails often breed on the brushy heath around the lakes. The Trail passes the south-eastern shore of the small lake system, then heads up towards Árdná. After walking a short distance through spruce forest you will arrive at a steep incline in drier birch forest. Here a strenuous climb awaits.

When you have passed the treeline, the view expands northwards, behind you, encompassing not only the Pite river valley, but high Ráskka (1456m) to the west. The rapids by the Pite bridges shine like white froth, surrounded by dark forest, and on the north shore of Tjieggelvas the buildings at Västerfjäll appear like little dots in the forest carpet. Single buildings can also be seen in other places. The forest along the north side of the valley also has large patches with dull greenery: pine grows here, offering a marked colour contrast to the pale green of the dominant birches.

Below Árdná the gradient levels out, but the terrain undulates between large boulders, areas of smaller stones, and willow thicket. It is rather trying terrain for the walker. The view includes the distinct Árdnavágge valley immediately to the west, which has the same terrain: this is untouched country where hardly anyone has ever set foot. The Trail now passes a reindeer herder's hut and continues to a bridge across the Tjävrra river to reach the Tjäura *kåtor*, which is built of peat. The hut can be used for an overnight stop.

Beyond the hut there is a steep and short hill, and not long after this, the Trail changes direction, turning south and heading diagonally up the long fell ridge of Barturtte. This slope is very smooth, with scanty ground cover: Three-leaved Rush (*Juncus trifidus*) is the predominant plant on the easily negotiated grass heath. As you climb, the view expands and with one glance you can get a summary of the geography of Lapland. The Pite river valley forms an oblong giant bowl in the middle of the landscape to the north. To the west, there is a high wall of majestic fells, while to the east there is a low area of flat forest ridges. Further east the view never seems to end as the eye takes in the vast

inland. Nearby, below the slope there is an area with many lakes, and
below this, in the bottom of the bowl, Tjieggelvas, with its two large
bays, glitters. The channel between the bays is not visible, but Lulep
Ramanj (720m) rises by the narrow waist of the lake, its sharp contours
showing clearly.

The views inspire a blissful feeling. Walking here, I find, is very
uplifting. The ascent is drawn out but not exceptionally tiring, and
you gradually approach historic ground. The German baron Daniel
August von Hogguér walked in this area in 1828, his guide the priest
and writer Petrus Læstadius who later became very well-known. In
their time, this was a *terra incognita*, and Barturtte is still a desolate part
of the fell world today.

On the other side of Barturtte a new view of immense proportions
opens up. To the west is Áksega (1398m), a rounded hill which is an
extension of the ridge you are walking on. And when you have passed
a level section of terrain called Gásaklahko ('the goose plain'), even
more of the western landscape becomes visible. Beside Áksega is the
much steeper summit of Lulep Gálddo (1187m). The peak plunges
down into a spacious basin filled by the large Bartávrre lake. Across the
water there is another high summit, Kietsekaise (1146m), which looks
like a petrified ocean wave among the ripples of the lower fells. From
Bartávrre, Kietsekaise soars up from a wide scree slope and a sheer rock
face.

In the south, the ante-fell terrain takes over, low birch forest areas
spreading out towards Riebnes lake, which one can only get a narrow
glimpse of, giving only a hint of its real size. A multitude of glittering
small lakes is scattered across the forest carpet stretching for many
kilometres in this direction. Some fell profiles can also be discerned.
Riebnesgáisse (1136m) is one of these, looking uncannily like
Kietsekaise and shaped like congealed surf. This type of profile is
common in the fells here and reflects the inclination of the projecting
rocks. At an even greater distance, about 35km away, you will now also
see for the first time Pieljekaise (1138m) with its saddle-like summit.

This is a landmark which will often crop up in this section of the Trail, and will also be seen during the subsequent stages.

The trail now descends towards Båråktjåhkkå (953m), a small thickset hillock on the slope. But before you get too close, I suggest you pitch your tent and enjoy the views. It is not difficult to find a good pitch here.

Day excursions

1. While you are here, why not explore the little known Arjeplog fells? You can saunter along the slope above Bartávrre towards Lulep Gálddo (1187m, the name means 'the east spring') and admire the views. Maintain altitude and aim for the summit of Änut (1007m) across terrain that is mostly easy to negotiate, with wide, constant views. Along both the near and far shores of Bartávrre there is a band of birch forest, while higher up there is a world of rarely visited low fells. The lake is teeming with fish. You can walk to a high cirque, surrounded by Lulep Gálddo and Áksega. Here, below the summits, the country is level, plateau-like, but with a sharp edge towards Bartávrre. The fell brook running through the cirque, Ahkágutjjåhkå, is sacred in Sámi tradition, as is the distinctive hillock of Viehtjer (1146m). From here there is also a good view south towards Kietsekaise whose summit is an isolated 600m high rock fortress with steep sides and a wavy plateau at the top.

If you climb Lulep Gálddo (which is best done from the north), the view towards the west expands, taking in the fortress of Gusstar (1627m), which is difficult to access: it has a 900m high and over 10km long rock face running north-west. The upper parts of the peak are a crumpled plateau with several high points. In the valley below, several lakes form a string of pearls, while in the far distance the high summits of Árjep Sávllo (1715m), Nuortta Sávllo (1762m) and Suliskongen in Sulitelma (1907m) can be seen.

Distance: about 24km. Height gain/loss: +300m (to Lulep Gálddo). Time: 10–12 hours.

16. Båråktjåhkkå − Vuonatjviken

**Distance: about 13km. Height gain/loss: -380m. Time: 4–6 hours.
Normal.**

*The stage start with a descent into the birch forest, still with extensive views.
The rest of the walk is through forest with more limited views. When close to
the day's objective you cross a beautiful forest river.*

The Trail continues downhill over open fell, steeply at first, passing a
faintly chiselled out depression between Båråktjåhkkå and the small,
bare Vuordnátj (770m). Eventually you reach the birch forest in the
Gåråkvágge valley. During the descent you will see the plateau of

Vuoktanj (1008m) on the other
side of the valley, a couple of
kilometres away. When you reach
the valley, the trees become
scarcer, subalpine heath opening
up: here there is often a pocket of
cold air, too harsh a climate for
birch. To the west of the Trail
there was once a Sámi settlement
where hay was made: it is possible
that haymaking also contributed to
keeping the birch sparse.

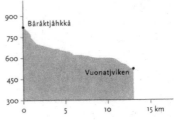

Now, for a short distance, you walk across open areas with Bååråktjåhkkå behind you like a high rocky hill. After crossing the bridge over Vilitjåhkå the Trail again enters a dense forest, with some wet areas. Continuing downhill, you cross the Arctic Circle (though, of course, there is nothing to see), and the trail becomes a bit harder to negotiate. It is stony, the terrain undulating, though it is still a fine experience to walk here in the depths of fell birch forest. You cross a reindeer fence, then stay close to Gåbdok lake. The view opens up again here, the twin-like summits of Kietsekaise and Riebnesgájsse being the main focus of attention.

The path next emerges onto a narrow strip of land between the Gåbdok and Lijgga lakes, and soon after you will cross a shallow inlet on a long *spång* (boardwalk). The strong gushing sound of the Bártek river can now be heard: you cross the cascading river on a suspension bridge a little further on. The Trail then climbs up a small ridge that runs beside the constantly roaring river. From the ridge you get good views again, seeing clearly all the prominent summits in the area. The Trail then re-enters dense forest, running through slightly hilly terrain past a few tarns to reach a prepared resting place by the river. The rest of the day's walking is easy, on dry ground through the pines, the houses in Vuonatjviken emerging with little forewarning.

Vuonatjviken

The homestead was founded by the Sámi Abram Johansson towards the end of the 19th century. Later Vuonatjviken was classed as a fell property, the State being the landowner. In the 1920s Vuonatjviken's isolation was broken and postal services became regular. At the same time telephone lines were installed, but there has never been a road. The most common way of reaching the village was, and still is, by boat from Riebnesluspen to the south-east. To get to the landing stage there, one was forced to get a boat across Hornavan and then to walk 5km through the forest from lake to lake, but today there is a road to Riebnesluspen. It was built when the Riebnes lake, which is part of the

Skellefte river water system, was dammed in 1974. The shore line below the buildings in Vuonatjviken and a beautiful haymaking meadow were then flooded. At the same time, the deeply cut inlet, which gave the homestead its name, became a part of the southern section of the lake, transformed into a large bay. As a result, the shore was exposed to the waves, and only a few islets remain of the large Vuotnatjnjárgga peninsula, which used to protect the inhabitants from the wind. The water level varies by up to 13m, which means that at low water level unsightly mud flats are revealed.

The old homestead has now grown into a little village, which blends well into the forest. The two resident families have a house each, Kietsekaise rising like a mighty mountain lump above the trees behind them. Nearer the shore there are some storerooms, and in the lake there is, among other things, a large boat that provides a safe crossing over the windswept lake. Accommodation is available in the form of self-catering units, and there is also a restaurant. Many of the visitors are fishermen who stay here for long periods. Walkers can hire boats for fishing in the lake.

The boat crossing of Riebness does not follow a timetable, so it is necessary to make arrangements on an individual basis. From Vuonatjviken you can also arrange transport across Hornavan, which you reach after the half an hour crossing of Riebnes and an approximately two hours' further walking. For those who walk the Royal Trail from south to north, the boat crossings over Hornavan and Riebnes have to be booked in Jäkkvik.

Day excursions

1. Fishing is the natural occupation during a day's rest in this area, but birdwatching by the collection of small lakes in the forest north of Vuonatjviken is also excellent. Here you will find plenty of waterfowl and, if you are lucky, you may see a White-tailed Eagle.

2. Kietsekaise (1146m) will provide satisfaction to walkers wanting to reach a summit. The name means 'the high narrow fell'. To climb the

peak I suggest that you initially follow the telephone line from Vuonatjviken to the Baurtaurluspe Sámi settlement about 8km away and then follow the Njásaválle ridge (*válle* means 'the smooth long sloping east end of a mountain') to the summit. As with other open summits, the view is phenomenal. The peak is a gigantic outlook tower offering a 360° view. Right down in the depths you can see Bartávrre lake, calmly inserted between the hillsides, while to the north across the lake, stands the bulky fortress of Gusstar (1627m). You can also discern the peaks of Sulitelma in the far distance.

Distance: about 28km. Height gain/loss: ±630m. Time: 10–12 hours.

17. Vuonatjviken – Jäkkvik

Distance: about 8km (walk to Hornavan), Height gain/loss: +280m, -360m. Time: about 2 hours. Normal.

After the boat crossing of Riebnes there is a steep climb to a plateau, which opens new vistas towards the south. The path continues down through a lush forest to Hornavan. Earlier there was a boat across that lake too, but a new path is now being made, which will make it possible to walk to Jäkkvikk.

The 20-minute crossing over Riebness can be choppy as the expanse of water is large and the west wind has free scope across it. In the immediate vicinity there is only one substantial peak, Riebnesgáisse (1136m), which stands with one foot in the water by the southern shore where you disembark. Along the northern part of the lake there are only some modest fell ridges on which pines grow in clumps. On the south side, where the Royal Trail continues, there is only fell birch, which points to the significant difference in climate between the two sides of the lake.

You will be landed on a stony, exposed shore below a locked shed. The path starts immediately with an arduous climb up Tjidtjakválle, a

Stuor Dáhtá, with Vallespiken and Tarrekaise in the background

Vindelälven flows in a birch-covered valley below Rävfjallet

The view towards the Laitaure delta from Skierffe, with the Tjaktjajaure reservoir in the background

Riehkiere from Sjnulttjie

Potatiskullen (Potato Hill), Ammarnäs

Crossing Stuorajåbba on the way to Ammarnäs. In the distance is Skebleskalet

Syterskalet from the east, with Norra Sytertoppen on the right

The land to the east of Norra Storfjället is important to reindeer herders. Please be considerate!

Bull Elk

Bluethroat

Redpoll

Looking east from Norra Sytertoppen

Syterskalet and Södra Sytertoppen

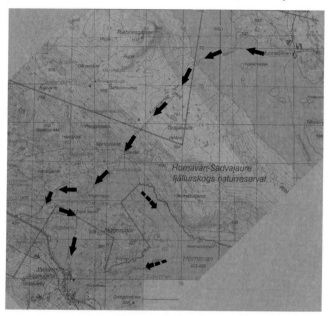

high ridge between the Riebnes and Hornavan lakes. The ascent is 300m, and at times the gradient is very sharp. At first the Trail runs parallel to a small brook: higher up you will cross an unusually well-defined treeline. Once out on the open heath, the Trail skirts around a couple of tarns, and the gradient decreases. If you pause for a rest here, look back to enjoy a marvellous view with Kietsekaise (1146m), Barturtte (1048m), Bååråktjåhkkå (953m) and Vuoktanj (1048m) all well-

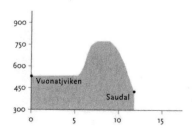

129

displayed. The Trail crosses a plateau with a beautiful mix of grass, low growing scrub and scattered junipers to reach Tjidjakvalle's highest point. Here, a broad view towards the south awaits. The nearest landmark in that direction is Pieljekaise (1138m), on the north side of which you can see a very long ski tow. If you let your eye pass along the horizon in a semi-circle, many more important summits can be counted. About 50km to the south, the east precipice of Riehkiere (1382m) stands out: the Royal Trail passes below this. Further towards the west are the two bulky peaks of Svájppá (1430m) and Ertektjåhkkå (1357m) in Laisdalen, while to the north-west the powerful dome of Tjidják (1587m) rises above the multitude of less distinctive lower fells.

The descent to Hornavan starts with a fairly flat downward slope: when you reach the well-defined treeline, follow a small brook. The ground is quite boggy in places, and further down, where the gradient increases, large pines become more common. You will soon lose contact with the brook: continue steeply downhill through the plant-abundant forest to reach the old settler's farmstead of Saudal. If there is anybody there, you can phone for a boat, but it is safer to pre-book the transport to Jäkkvik while you are in Vuonatjviken. In strong winds the boat crossing may be curtailed: in that case the crossing will end at Lövmokk where the old chapel used to be positioned.

However, an extension of the Royal Trail is now being waymarked from Saudal to Jäkkvik. The path will be made along the shore of Hornavan to the rapids between Harrselet and Tjårvekallegiehtje, where a rowing route will be prepared, with boats on both sides. The path will then continue past Lövmokk and along the eastern shore of Jäggávrre southwards to Jäkkvik. The path will be about 10km long.

JÄKKVIK -

Distance: 83km. Height gain/loss:

This section of the Royal Trail is also surprisingly little used by the walkers. As in the area north of Jäkkvik, the landscape is characterised by a regular mix of fell plateaux and forest country, the Trail taking the walker from one river valley to another, crossing the low fells that separate them. From Jäkkvik the Trail heads over Pieljekaise to an overnight hut located in the National Park, which shares the name. In the Park, and all the way to Adolfsström, you are surrounded by the largest and most lush fell birch forests along the Trail. Accommodation is available in Adolfsström. Alternatively you can carry on to Bäverholmen, using a boat to cross Iraft lake. Accommodation is also available in Bäverholmen.

On the stretch from Bäverholmen to Ammarnäs, the landscape becomes more varied, the Trail traversing forested valleys and crossing extensive fell plateaux. The Trail enters Laisdalen briefly, then climbs to an extensive plateau of alternating fell heath and birch forest, with many lakes and bogs in a mosaic-like mix. The plateau is almost entirely surrounded by rounded fell ridges, giving it the feeling of a

– AMMARNÄS

+1740m, -1670m. Time: 6–7 days.

crater. This is the Svaipa Bird Reserve, set up to protect the abundant bird life: somewhere around here you will need to camp overnight.

The next day walk offers a marked change in scenery. The Trail continues across the plateau past a large moraine bank below the precipitous Låddievárdduo, and then climbs steeply up to the prairie-like expanses of Björkfjället. Up there, on the boundary between Norrbotten and Västerbotten, there are good places to camp if you wish to shorten the day's walk. From here *Kungsleden* used to head due south through the Vindelfjällen Nature Reserve to Ammarnäs, but the Trail now turns north-west and crosses the long southern slope of Björkfjället to reach the narrow and fertile Vindelådalen where there is a hut that can be used. At Rävfjallet ('fox fall') the Trail crosses a bridge over Vindelälven and climbs to the long fell ridge of Stuorajåbba, then runs parallel to the awe-inspiring precipices of Ammarfjället, to the west. The bird life is exceptionally abundant here. Finally, the Trail descends steeply to Ammarnäs village.

18. Jäkkvik – Pieljekaise

Distance: about 8km. Height gain/loss: +360m, -90m. Time: 3–4 hours. Easy.

A short stage: a prolonged ascent through lush birch forest is followed by the crossing of a fell plateau, with the summit of Pieljekaise as a constant landmark.

It is easy to find the starting point in Jäkkvik: by Silvervägen (road No. 95) there is a signpost for the Royal Trail. From a car park, the path enters a damp birch forest with a wonderful display of flowers, including Northern Wolfsbane (*Aconitum septentrionale*), Globeflower (*Trollius europeus*) and Lesser Stitchwort (*Stellaria graminea*). After a short distance you cross a brook, and the Trail steepens. The forest is still lush, but gradually thins and takes on a drier and brighter character, with carpets of Oak Fern (*Gymnocarpium dryopteris*) in the undergrowth.

When you reach the treeline, there is a small hut about 100m from the trail. It is open for resting and cooking, but is not intended for overnight stays. Behind the hut, to the west, the landscape forms a large, mainly forested hollow with Tjáhtsáljáurátj lake at its centre. The forest covers the slopes all the way up to the surrounding fell ridges beyond the lake, the silhouetted trees high on the edge giving the topography a thrilling scale. The view north, behind you, is very extensive, the main landmark being Riebnesgáijsse (1136m), which has an abrupt ledge towards the east, like a frozen breaker on the sea. In the front of the peak is a large, slightly undulating depression. This is the wide Skellefte river valley. Between the hills, in the dense coniferous forest carpet down in the valley you can also see the west end of the Hornavan lake, as well as Jäkkvik village and Silvervägen (the Silver Road).

Just above the treeline you reach a path fork, where a path takes off due south aiming for Viejenäs 15km away. In that direction Pieljekaise (1138m, the name means 'the mountain that looks like a dog's ear'), a

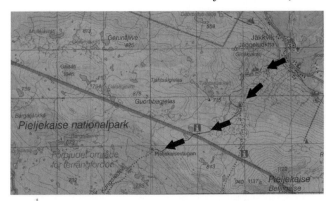

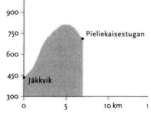

sacred peak to the Sámi, dominates the view. It has two distinctive summits with a saddle between: the upper part of the peak is surprisingly rocky for such a low summit. On the northern summit (1122m) there is a small building.

Often, as far as the path fork you will meet other walkers on day trips from Jäkkvik, but beyond it the fell is usually deserted. The Trail continues to climb, heading diagonally south-west to reach a low hill. The scrub heath is wet at first, but becomes drier as you climb. Distant peaks also appear ahead, the view becoming as extensive to the south as it is northwards when you reached the high point on the wide fell plateau west of Pieljekaise. Only the peak prevents a 360° panorama.

The absence of competing peaks makes Pieljekaise a more majestic mountain than its altitude might indicate. Looking west, Laisdalen acts as a good guideline for orienting your view of the high peaks to the south side. Svájppa (1430m) and Ertektjåhkkå (1357m) are easy to identify with, behind them, 50km away, the more pointed summit of

Tsángátjåhkkå (1641m). A remarkable peak closer to you is Kráhpiesvárrie (1079m): the name means 'the mountain with rough terrain, small cliffs and clefts', and this is very apt, as it has a long hunchback with many mini-summits that create a scraggy profile which stands out sharply just under 20km away. About double that distance in the same direction you can also see the abrupt eastern precipice of Riehkiere (1382m), another good landmark.

The Trail now enters the Pieljekaise National Park, one of the least known in Sweden. It was established in 1909 and was originally a small area, just 200 hectares, but was expanded three years later to its present size of 14,600 hectares. The main purpose of the Park was protection of a large fell birch forest. Thanks to the protection, the Park is now one of the most unspoiled areas in Sweden for this type of forest. At the Park boundary there is an information board. From the boundary the Trail descends into a valley at the heart of the Park, with a view to the vertical peak of Báktek (788m). In the valley you reach an open forest with a rich flora: beyond a short, grassy climb the Trail bears west to reach the Pieljekaise hut, hidden by birches and set beside a noisy brook.

Pieljekaise hut (710m)

The hut at Pieljekaise is in the care of the local County Council. Its large room is at the disposal of walkers taking a break and is unlocked. However, the sleeping accommodation is locked. If you intend to use the hut for an overnight stop you will need to obtain a key from the Ica shop in Jäkkvik or the shop in Adolfsström: there is a charge for the key. Walkers who borrow the key in Jäkkvik must drop it off in Adolfsström (and vice versa). The hut has a Calorgas stove and a gas lamp. One curiosity is the large Elk antler rack with 19 points hanging on the wall. The rack was found near the hut in 1987: the large bull it belonged to had been killed in a rutting fight. The ground around the hut is steep and decking has been constructed around the log shed. The local terrain is an undulating field of large boulders. Between the trees you can just see the top of the small but steep Báktek (788m).

Day excursions

1. Pieljekaise is an attractive viewpoint and a worthwhile objective. Follow *Kungsleden* back to the open fell and continue across the heath towards the western precipice, climbing this to reach a substantial cairn and a limitless panorama. Because the peak is strikingly isolated, nothing obscures the view. In clear weather you can see almost all of the prominent summits of Arjeplog. To the north is Gusstar (1627m), more north-west is Tjidják (1587m), to the west is Fierrás (1599m), to the south-west the two 'body-guards' of Laisdalen, Ertektjåhkkå (1357m) and Svájppá (1430m), while further away in the same direction is unmistakable Riehkiere (1382m). A long line of snow-covered peaks in Sarek and Sulitelma sparkle to the far north, while to the east the vast rolling forest country spreads out. Large parts of Hornavan can also be seen, though it is difficult to make out the shape of the lake. Much closer, there is a view over the Pieljekaise National Park, which you can now place in its geographical context. The protected area has widespread birch forests, many small hills and patchy lakes, forming an interesting mix. The trail to Viejenäs cuts through the forest like a line.

From the summit it is best to descend down the southern side to the small lake at 853m. The lake is beautifully situated in a bowl and has excellent camping spots. From the lake head diagonally back to *Kungsleden* and the hut.

Distance: about 12km. Height gain/loss: ±430m. Time: 5–7 hours.

2. Another viewpoint of the National Park is Báktek (788m). Although the view is not as extensive, as the peak is closer to the heart of the Park, it offers a closer view, richer in detail. Follow *Kungsleden* south, down into the valley and over a bridge, then turn off south-east through the forest and climb to the bare peak. To the north the mountain has a dizzying 80m precipice, beneath which lies the central valley of the Park, framed by the wide southern side of Pieljekaise fell. In other directions an undulating forest country spreads out. Far off to the west, well-known peaks such as Svájppá can be seen. The most

eye-catching feature on the horizon are the two camel-humps of Tjårrås (1036m) on Kráhpiesvárrie. On the valley ridges the forest is denser than in the hollows where there are open bogs: a vast number of boulders lie scattered about the whole area. To the east, the forest country is vast, its wilderness character gilded by the Bieljávrre lakes appearing like a bright arrow 20km away. In Jutis, by Silvervägen, you will be able to make out a tall chimney.

Báktek is also an excellent spot for game watching. The fauna of the National Park is exciting: Wolverine and Golden Eagle are regular inhabitants, and large Elk bulls may also be seen in the valley.

19. Pieljekaise – Adolfsström

Distance: about 14km. Height gain/loss: +180m, -380m. Time: 4–6 hours. Normal.

This stage goes through the Pieljekaise National Park, across some open bogs, but mostly being within a large fell birch forest with occasional lakes.

Beyond the hut, the Trail is rather stony and arduous as it follows the valley through the National Park towards the forested ridge west of Báktek. In the central valley, the Trail crosses a number of open heaths and bogs, the trees becoming both scarce and small so that the landscape is, in place, almost scrub. A bridge is used to cross a small brook: there is a latrine by the bridge. From the bridge you can see Pieljekaise, but otherwise it is fell birch forest as far as the eye can see.

On the other side of the valley, an arduous climb passes a little tarn. Apart from the dry birch forest, the area is botanically poor, though at one point a small, isolated group of spruce has taken root. Further on the going is eased by a descent towards Luvtávrre lake, situated in a hollow completely surrounded by slopes covered with dense birch forest. Here the Trail has been re-routed. Originally it went to the

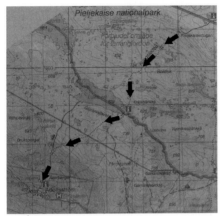

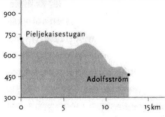

middle of the lake where it could be rowed, but now it bears south to the lakes' outlet where there is a bridge and another latrine.

Before reaching the bridge you walk along a ridge, which allows a view of Luvtávrre in its entirety. At the bridge the Trail leaves the National Park and starts a long climb over Gárránistjavelg ('the raven's back'). The Trail now passes through a monotonous, dry area: kilometre after kilometre there is nothing but the same tree species and level terrain. No hills to provide variation, no views over the trees. The area feels impenetrable, as if you really have been utterly absorbed by the forest. If the air is still, the only sound is the crunch of last year's leaves beneath your feet. But in spite of the monotony the forest has a bright character, and there is something of the Garden of Eden in its radiance, so that rather than being oppressive, the forest is restful.

After about 4km circumstances do change, the forest becoming more fertile, with tall plants in the undergrowth. The Trail also starts to descend, a small brook runs parallel to the path, and the vegetation along it forms a moist green ribbon in the forest. The gradient increases, becoming a steep downhill slope and over the tree tops you regain distant views, Ertektjåhkkå and Kráhpiesvárrie re-appear, their profiles easily recognised. The path descends into a hollow where Ráhpaájågåtj is crossed by a bridge. Beyond the bridge the Trail climbs, but only for a short distance. It then becomes wider, then turns into a forest road and reaches a fork: the Trail follows the western branch. Now the forest has both pine and birch, the terrain undulating until another desent is reached. The twin humps of Tjårras appear, as does Tjeäksá (1092m), the latter another peak reminiscent of a wave on the sea. And finaly you reach Adolfsström by a courtyard beside the main road. There are several possibilities for accommodation in the village.

Adolfsström (465m)

Adolfsström is located at the east shore of the Iraft lake and is the gateway to the Arjeplog fells. In spite of its remote location and its barren nature, the place has been inhabited since the end of the 18th century when people arrived to exploit the silver ore on Nasa fell. There had been other attempts at mining over the previous hundred years, but this was a more intensive attempt, a smelting plant being built, which laid the foundation for the village. The availability of pine for fuel and timber was crucial for the choice of Adolfsström as the site of the smelter, and to attract labour land was cleared for cultivation. Building started in 1773, Major Georg Bogislaus Staél von Holstein being the driving force behind the project. Under his leadership extensive drainage of bogs and meadows was carried out, but the work was not a success, the Major's efforts leaving the village destitute. The mining was not as successful as had been hoped either, and by 1814 there was little left of the smelting works. Seven years later what did remain burned down. As a result of the collapse of mining, the Swedish King decided that the settlements in Adolfsström should be transferred to State ownership, though property owners did retain some rights of possession, and those who wished could buy the homesteads. State ownership laid the foundation for a more permanent population in the village.

In fact, Adolfsström offered relatively good conditions for the people who stayed and moved in. The alluvial plain of the Lais river delta in Iraft lake was perfect land for haymaking and cultivation and a small agricultural community developed there with barns and meadows, which are still there today. The area has now been set aside as a Nature Reserve, annual haymaking has been maintained, the numerous small barns scattered on the islets of the delta being picturesque memorials of a traditional way of life.

Today, Adolfsström is a quiet village at the end of the road. The villagers today live mainly by tourism, many having huts and cabins for hire. There is also a shop where you return (or hire) the key for the Pieljekaise hut. The stream of tourists in the summer is still comparatively small, but during late winter there are many more visitors, mostly here for the fishing and to drive snowmobiles. There is a small airport where helicopter flights can be organised. The area around the village is very wild depsite the mountains being fairly low.

In Laisälven valley the country is hilly, with precipitous mountains, rock ledges and boulders along the valley sides. Pine grow high up on the crests of many of the hills, with open fell above these forest silhouettes. Geologically the area is also interesting: Kráhpiesvárrie, for instance, is composed of sparagmite, a Pre-Cambrian sandstone matrix with feldspar and quartz.

Day excursions

1. The old silver smelting-house has now been restored. It is located by the brook between Lárvvejávre and Iraft, and is reached along a path from the road at the edge of the village. The watermill and smithy have been rebuilt. Major von Holstein's house in the village also remains from that short industrial period.

2. Märkberget is a place of botanical interest 10km east of Adolfsström along the road. Try to arrange a lift there as the round trip is very long. From the top of the hill you will get a magnificent view of the wilderness, with Sikselet lake down in a bowl below the tall

Kráhpiesvárrie (1004m). The thundering Märkforsen river discharges into the lake after running through a narrow ravine. The easiest route to the rapids is an old, boggy path from the road. To the east another interesting spot is the Märkklyftan ravine, which is about 30m deep and 200m long and was created at the last Ice Age by gushing meltwater. Today there is only a tiny stream at the bottom. The south side of Märkberget is a so-called southern plant hill where you will find both sunlit screes, small rock precipices and shaded deciduous woodlands. The topography and geology make the vegetation rich, and you may come across Common Kidney-Vetch (*Anthyllis vulneraria*), Hairy Rockcress (*Arabis hirsuta*), Herb Paris (*Paris quadrifolia*), Alpine Enchanter's Nightshade (*Circaea alpina*), Lady's Slipper Orchid (*Cypripedium calceolus*), *Polemoniacae acutiflorum* (a rare form of Jacob's Ladder), Great-spurred (or Selkirk's) Violet (*Viola selkirkii*), Holly Fern (*Polystichum lonchitis*), Oblong Woodsia (*Woodsia ilvensis*) and Ostrich Fern (*Matteucia struthiopteris*) – to mention only a few of the more nutrient-demanding plants.

3. On the south side of Iraft, Tjeäksá (1092m) is an enticing viewpoint ,which also has a rich flora. The mountain was called Tjäktja ('osprey') on old maps, the new name deriving from the nodular third stomach of a reindeer, perhaps because the peak is part of the same ridge as the knobbly Kráhpiesvárrie. Arrange a boat crossing in Adolfsström and ask to be put ashore on the south side of Laisälven, by a windshield upstream from Bäverholmen (' beaver islet'), but on the opposite side of the river. From there you can follow a path straight up the north side of the peak, where you may spot the rare Alpine Arnic (*Arnica alpina*). The view from the peak towards the delta in Iraft is magnificent.

Distance: about 8km. Height gain/loss: ±630m. Time: about 3–4 hours.

20. Adolfsström – Sjnulttjie

Distance: about 23km (15km from Bäverholmen). Height gain/loss: +400m, -100m. Time: 5–7 hours. Strenuous.

You can save yourself some distance by taking a boat to Bäverholmen. From there the trail just touches Laisdalen before it climbs to the not easily surveyable landscape in the Svaipa Bird Sanctuary, where lakes, bogs and groves are interspersed with open heath.

The road in Adolfsström ends at the Iraft jetties. From there, the Royal Trail continues along the north shore of the lake, but if you wish to save yourself an 8km shore-line walk, take the boat to Bäverholmen. The crossing can be booked in the village shop.

The path along the north shore of Iraft is not very clear in places, but is well worth taking for the lovely views across the water towards Tjeäksá, at the base of which there are a number of barns. The Trail runs alternately in the forest and along the shore. On the water you will probably see several species of waterfowl, including Black-throated Diver, Red-breasted Merganser, Common Goldeneye, Wigeon, Velvet Scoter and Scaup. Birch is the predominant tree species in the forest, but pines still define its character. After just over a kilometre you follow a telephone line, then walk down to the lake where there is a rest place.

After a further few kilometres the Trail turns away from the lake, crossing a tongue of land to reach the small Bietsek lake. Now skirt around Ahaviken, an inlet of Iraft (the name means 'narrow inlet'), to reach dense forest. Here the terrain is undulating and stony, but the ground is dry: pines with suspended lichen become quite a feature of the walk here. A short descent completes the walk to Bäverholmen where you reach a delightful haymaking meadow in the middle of which there is a large building serving refreshments. Close by, near the river, there is a house, and on the forested slope above the meadow there are several small overnight huts. There is a jetty with boats by the river. These items comprise this small tourist village far out in

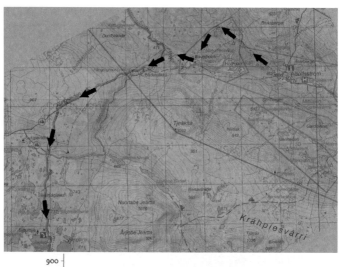

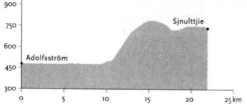

roadless country. There is a restaurant and accommodation, and boat trips can be arranged. You can also hire a canoe and obtain a key to the Rävfjallet hut. The Laisälven river is huge here and flows sedately past Bäverholmen. As the village's name ('beaver home') suggests, there are numerous traces of beaver, mainly felled trees. Far away in the east you can see Kráhpiesvárrie, but the most prominent mountain is Tjeäksá, which rises boldly on the other side of the river.

From Bäverholmen, walk upstream along the river bank. As the river bends, the path follows the outer curve where there has been significant

144

erosion, some of the trees on the bank threatening to fall over. When the water level is high, the path and the *spångs* you are using become flooded. Beyond the bend, turn away from the riverbank to reach a small glade with a couple of picturesque barns. The vegetation is lush here, with Arctic Bramble (*Rubus arcticus*) growing near the path. When you rejoin the river, the current is very strong, and ahead you can see the impressive rapids under a suspension bridge that the Trail crosses. Here the landscape looks more valley-like than earlier, not least because Svájppa (1430m) appears ahead. The summit has a relatively long ridge curving elegantly down towards Laisdalen. Behind, downstream, Tjeäksá now forms a wider, more moderate high ridge.

By the bridge there is a fork in the path. Straight ahead the path continues through Laisdalen to Kattuggleselet ('Tawny Owl water'), but the Royal Trail crosses and heads diagonally through the forest to Bárasjuhka, a large tributary of the Laisälven. The tributary carries a large volume of water and forms a continuous string of cascades as it plunges down the hills. On the banks of the tributary, and on small islets in the river, there are lush meadows, with many tall plants. The Trail passes several sites among the pines, which would make ideal camp sites before reaching, after about a kilometre, a bridge over Bárasjuhka. Here the river comes out of a deep, very long, north–south river-cut ravine with steep sides. On the hill, just above the opening of the ravine, there is a hut, well hidden in the forest, which can be used for a rest. Beyond the hut, you leave the last few pines and enter birch forest.

Just before the spot where the Trail is crossed by an overhead powerline, look for an old pit about 20m into the forest to the right. The pit is about 2m deep and 3m in diameter and is likely to date from the Middle Ages when the Sámi hunted, rather than herded, Reindeer. The pit would have been lined with sharp poles, Reindeer being manoeuvred towards the pit in the hope that one or more would fall in. It is known that this area was important stage on the Reindeer's annual migration, large herds passing through. Similar pits are also found in other places along the migration routes, for instance below

Tjeäksá. Beyond the pit, the Trail steepens all the way to the treeline, where the view opens out. To the north, behind you, is Pieljekaise, the isolated peak again being a significant landmark, its profile unmistakable. Interestingly, the double summit looks almost the same from this direction as it does from north of Jäkkvik. Iraft lake can also be seen from here.

The fell heath ahead provides easy walking, the Trail rising slowly towards a crest where the view southwards opens up of a landscape that is both exciting and bewildering. The terrain is broken, with bare hills and clumps of birch forest alternating with open bogs. There is also a multitude of lakes of different sizes. This natural mosaic fills an enormous bowl encircled by rounded fell ridges. Two summits stand out in this circle of mountains. Riehkere (1382m, the name means 'broken sledge') is the most prominent peak, characterised by a long level summit ridge with an abrupt ledge towards the east. The second is Láddievárdduo (1111m, its name meaning 'the stranger's viewpoint'), which has a broad rock face at one end of a high plateau. Both peaks are associated with Sámi legends about the 'tether people' who were said to be cruel strangers who always approached in groups, threatening the Sámi people.

To the east, the landscape is calmer. The famous Tjeäksá summit appears as a high protuberance on a long fell ridge. The south-east side slopes down towards a nameless forested valley in the middle of which a small, inviting lake glistens like a bird's eye. On the opposite side of the valley is Nuortab Jeärtta (1076m), its summit forming the northernmost crest of a crumpled low fell massif, set like a bare island in the forest in the nameless valley.

The Trail now crosses an open plain, allowing contemplation of these various views for about 4km until it again enters the birch forest, continuing to reach a second bridge over Bárasjuka, which here flows due east. The forest floor is initially level, with beautiful grass ridges, but as the river is approached there are several steep downhill sections. Close to the river the terrain is free from trees and is very boggy, Bárasjuka draining large lakes further west and so often having a very high volume flow. If you have time, about a kilometre upstream of the bridge, by the Svájpavallie Sámi settlement, there are some rapids, which are well worth seeing.

Beyond the bridge the Trail climbs slightly into a new forest area, passing a small lake with, for a backdrop, the arrogant outline of Riehkere. There is now a surprisingly long stretch through the forest, many of the trees being young saplings, as the Trail climbs over a hill. When Plassuoke lake is reached the Trail follows a long ridge, then a stony and arduous path past Stårbmiejávrrie lake: several species of waterfowl can often be seen on the lakes. You are now close to the site of the Sjnulttjie hut, which I suggest is a reasonable destination for this stage. The hut used to be located about 500m west of the Royal Trail, but burned down in 2005. A new shelter is planned for the same site, but even after it has been built, I recommend that you carry a tent on this section of the Trail to give greater freedom in organising the stage.

Alternative path

There is an alternative path from Laisälven to Sjnulttjie, one which is a lightly shorter, but which involves more forest walking. The route starts from the south bank of the Laisälven and heads, initially, towards Tjeäksá before turning along the slope to the west of the summit. After walking briefly on open fell the route goes steeply downhill through the birch forest to reach the point where the Bárasjuka river bends sharply to the north. From here a path continues through the forest and eventually reaches the mosaic-like fell area around Sjnulttjie.

Distance: about 13km (from Bäverholmen). Height gain/loss: +460m, -160m. Time: 4–6 hours.

Sjnulttjie

Sjnulttjie is situated 200m north of lake Suolojávrrie ('the island lake') in an area of damp scrub heath sloping down towards the lake shore. The view covers a semi-circular panorama from east to south to west, a forested hill obscuring the view northwards. The local landscape has a very special character, looking a little like a huge crater: you stand in the centre of this, with, just over 10km away, an enclosing circle of high ridges forming the crater rim. The only dramatic landforms within view are the eastern precipices of Láddievárdduo and Riehkiere. On the whole the ground is not too good for camping, but you can pitch a tent next to a large boulder close to the lake.

Day excursions

1. The area around Sjnulttjie is an excellent base for birdwatching, the great mix of differing natural features making the birdlife rich. Many species of waterfowl and waders can be found, as well as a number of passerines. Ahájávrrie (meaning 'the lake with inlets') is one of several possible destinations for an excursion. The shore habitat around this lake consists of scrub heaths and bogs, and you may spot the very rare Lesser White-fronted Goose. On the water, you are likely to see, for example, Black-throated Diver, Long-tailed Duck, Scaup, Velvet Scoter and Common Gull. Birds of prey passing through regularly are Rough-legged Buzzard, Gyrfalcon, Merlin, Golden Eagle, White-tailed Eagle and Hen Harrier.

2. A destination close at hand for the walker wishing to get a good geographical overview of the area is Deärmbietjåhkka (828m), to the west, from where you will see large parts of the 'crater caldera'. To get there, follow the northern shores of Suolojávrrie and Deärbmiejávrrie, then climb steep through the forest to the summit. To the north, Deärmbietjåhkka is hilly. The bedrock there is interesting and belongs to the middle nappe, which geologists call the Gavas window after Gávasjávrrie lake. This middle rock was for a long time covered by an upper strata from which the large fell area further west is made, but after hundreds of millions of years of weathering, the upper rock layers have been worn away. The Gavas window can be regarded as a peephole down through the fell bedrock. The middle nappe strata consists of sandstone and granite, which are hard and acidic, and do not form a soil favourable to plant life. The compensation is the way the flat rocks glisten in the undulating terrain.

Beyond Gávasjávrrie to the north, the high summit of Svájppá (1430m) forms a very broad fell. In the depression below it lie the Tjålmiejávrrie lakes, while further away to the west several high fell massifs can be seen. To the south-west, at a distance of only 5km, is the precipice of Riehkiere (1382m): this is the most sharply defined outline in the whole view. The nearer Gávastjåhkka (1029m) also has a steep precipice above the small Báktasjávrrie lake.

3. Why not carry on? Westwards from Deärmbietjåhkka you can aim for Riehkere, climb to its summit. To get there you will first have to ford the brook near Báktasjávrrie. Beyond, skirt around the high north-eastern precipice of Riehkiere to reach the bowl between this summit and Dåriestjåhkka (1289m). Heaths with short grass and, higher up, patches of snow cover the ground here. The route to the summit is easy to negotiate. In parts the vegetation is rich, the flora including Mountain Avens (*Dryas octopetala*). The Riehkiere bedrock includes limestone and therefore does not belong to the Gavas window, the limestone explaining the richer flora. In this vicinity an interesting archaeological find was made in 1644. On the moss carpet of the fell, two miners from Nasafjäll found a beautiful brass bridal crown. It is now kept in the Silver Museum in Arjeplog. According to legend the crown was dropped during a battle between Sámi and the 'Tethers', the robber band that occasionally marauded the Sámi, as already mentioned above.

Riehkiere offers an outstanding panorama. The summit has quite a narrow ridge stretching just over 2km towards the south-west, where another peak forms a corner in the massif. From there the ridge continues north-west, and the whole of Riehkiere therefore forming a triangular fortress. The view from the upper part of the peak is exceptional, stretching 100km northwards to Tarrekaise (1828m) and Bårddetjåhkkå (2005m) in Sarek, and 60-80km to the south and south-west as far as Norra Storfjället (1767m), Ammarfjället (1611m) and Oxtindarna (1915m), on the Norwegian side of the border. There are also good views of the interesting depression in the north, where the

Tjålmiejávrrie lakes form a complex water system. Above these you will see Tsángátjåhkka (1641m), which has an unexpectedly pointed peak.

From the highest point on Riehkiere you can, contrary to expectation, walk straight down the awe-inspiring southern precipice. This abrupt slope is divided into grass ledges with a rich flora, and you walk from ledge to ledge – though it is hard work, and you have to negotiate a scree slope further down: you may spot Ring Ouzels here. Below the precipice is the Vuorek plateau, a very interesting bird habitat, while the low-growing scrub and grass heath makes the going easy especially as the ground is unusually stone-free, and interest is maintained by a series of small lakes. The plateau has a rolling topography, and is framed by the high barrier of Riehkiere to the north-west and the rounded high points of Láddievárdduo (1111m) and Vuorátjåhkka (1244m) in the east and west. The bird life includes several species of wader, including Purple Sandpiper, Temminck's Stint, Dunlin, Red-necked Phalarope, Ringed Plover and Dotterel. Even the rare, and skulking, Shore Lark breeds here.

On the return route towards Sjnulttjie you walk down the northern slope of the plateau, with a good view of the crater caldera and *Kungsleden*. At Vuoruojuhka there are large bogs and willow thicket, where Great Snipe can be seen, as well as other waders. Now walk back to the bridge across the river and follow *Kungsleden* back to Sjnulttjie.

Distance: about 25km (whole trip). Height gain/loss: ±720m. Time: about 10–12 hours (whole trip).

4. Tjålmiejávrrie (meaning 'the breezy lake') is another very rewarding destination for birdwatchers. Walk around the south side of Deärmbietjåhkka and then over mostly easy fell heath to the southern tip of Gávasjávrrie ('the curved lake'). Above the shore there are small clumps of fell birch. As you progress towards Gierduosjávrrie the terrain becomes more scrubby and bogs spread out ahead of you, making walking harder work – but if you are birdwatching you should walk

slowly anyway. The lake forms an inlet in the complex lake system in the valley, the mix of fell plain and water creating a confusing landscape mosaic with a rich biology. The whole area is set apart as the Svaipa Bird Sanctuary (where waterfowl hunting is banned). The lake system is broken up by a conglomerate archipelago with around 75 islets, the depression the system occupies being large and surrounded by sturdy and gradually sloping fell massifs. The islets are built up of rogen moraine ridges. These are formed beneath, and transverse to the flow of, a glacier or advancing ice sheet: the best known area of this terrain is at Rogenryggen by Lake Rogen at Anåkröken in central Sweden, which are the 'type-form' and have given the form its name. Here, at Svaipa, the islets are shaped like parallel land tongues, 10–15m high. The archipelago has protected breeding places for waterfowl, while the shallow lakes provide good nourishment. Many species are regularly found here: Black-throated Diver, Red-throated Diver, Goosander, Red-breasted Merganser, Long-tailed Duck, Scaup, Common Scoter, Velvet Scoter, Northern Pintail, Wigeon, Mallard and Teal. Lesser White-fronted Geese has one of its last strongholds in the fells here. The boggy and scrubby vegetation to the south and north of the lakes is also an excellent habitat for birds, several waders and small birds breeding here, the more unusual species including Red-throated Pipit.

On the way back it is worth climbing Gávastjåhkka (1029m): this means a 300m climb, but the view is excellent, particularly of the Tjålmejaure valley. Alternatively you can skirt round the peak and head in the direction of Riehkiere. Below the small precipice from the eastern ridge of Dåriestjåhkka (1289m) there is a well-developed meadow with several tall plant species, making it well worth visiting. The flora is rich with Globeflower (*Trollius europaeus*), Meadow Buttercup (*Ranunculus acris*), Angelica (*Angelica archangelica*), Northern Wolfsbane (*Aconitum septentrionale*), Red Campion (*Silene dioica*), Wood Cranesbill (*Geranium sylvaticum*), Drooping, Hairy and Yellow Mountain Saxifrage (*Saxifraga cernua, S. pubescens* and *S. aizodes*), Net-leaved Willow (*Salix reticulata*) and others. Having enjoyed the plant life it is best to continue past little, crystal-clear Báktasjávrrie lake below the southern slope of Gávastjåhkka and then to head straight back to Sjnulttjie.

Distance: about 23km (going past Dårestjåkkå). Height gain/loss: ±300m. Time: 8–10 hours.

21. Sjnulttjie – Rävfjället

Distance: about 25km. Height gain/loss: +260m, -520m. Time: 8–10 hours. Strenuous.

On this stage you will trek from the Arjeplog fells to the Vindel fells. The path leaves a mosaic landscape with indistinct features, follows a long moraine ridge and climbs up to the watershed on the Björkfjället plateau. With new views ahead, you then descend into the Vindelälven valley.

The path from the hut links up with the Royal Trail in a small clump of birches. Then, after 500m you will arrive at a forest edge, continuing across fell heath down to a minor brook flowing between Suoluojávrrie and Áhájávrrie. Here there is an open view across Áhájávrrie and the low scrubby shore area around it. Several privately owned huts can be seen on the other side of the water. By the brook the flora is visibly richer, an oasis in this otherwise botanically poor area. Among the plants you will find Alpine Meadow-rue (*Thalictrum alpinum*), Scottish Asphodel (*Tofieldia calyculata*), Net-leaved Willow (*Salix reticulata*) and Finely-toothed Willow (*Salix breviserrata*). Riehkiere dominates the landscape ahead.

Beyond the brook, the Trail ascends slightly to a small, tree-covered hill, then descends into an open depression, before climbing to another tree-clad hill. Look behind you here and you will see that Suolojávrrie has come into view. There is now a fork in the path. The old, increasingly overgrown, path of *Kungsleden* continues straight on here, through a scrubby and wet area, across most of which dwarf birches are knee-high. The new path of the Trail makes a wide sweep on drier

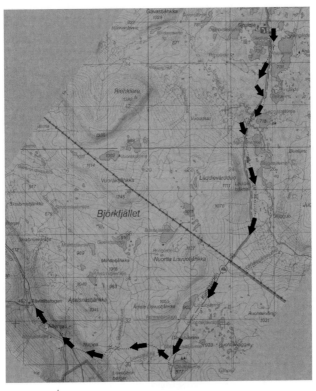

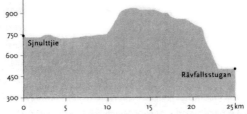

153

ground past a pointed little hill, a better route on easier ground. The Trail then continues in a wide curve back eastwards and follows a ridge, still dry underfoot, before making another wide sweep towards the south-west before resuming the original direction to reach a high point with a good view over the hollow around Vuoruojuhka.

The Trail now descends slightly to reach a bridge. Parallel to the path, on the left (east) there is a shallow valley with steep sides: this is an old furrow chiselled out by Ice Age meltwater. By the bridge across Vuoruojuhka there are some large sedge bogs, the river forging a winding course through the wet areas. Here, again, the birdlife is rich, with waders such as Snipe and Red-necked Phalarope often being seen. Prominent in the landscape are Láddievárdduo, to the south, and Riehkiere, to the west. Far away to the north-west Tsángátjåhkka (1641m) appears like a pyramid above the low fell ridges.

From the bridge you walk slightly uphill again and, at the same time, the Trail swings around towards the south-east and heads towards the precipice on Láddievárdduo. Ahead you will see the relatively large Njallabliehkie lake. The lake used to be called Seitejaure, as by its shore there were said to have been sacrificial sites with sacred stones (*seitar*). Also ahead, a high moraine ridge will catch your attention: the Trail heads towards this, then keeps below the ridge for a couple of kilometres. I suggest, however, that you walk straight up on to the ridge, as the walking along it is interesting. The ridge looks like a long rubble heap, and you might expect that it is as high on the side towards the precipice as towards the Trail. But this is not the case, something which becomes clear when you have climbed the 25m to the highest point. The inside is only 2 to 3m high and merges into a wide terrace, which joins up with the scree slope below Láddievárdduo. The surface of the terrace is full of water-filled holes. A moraine ridge of this kind is unusual in the fells (there is a similar one further on along *Kungsleden* below Stuvbiebákttie in Ammarfjället), and this one has a remarkable origin. Researchers think that it has been built up against a mass of ice that remained for a long time in the middle of the valley. Through earth slips and landslides on Láddievárdduo, earth and gravel were brought down towards the ice edge. Then, when this ice disappeared, the outer edge of the moraine ridge towards the valley became exposed. The lakes on the upper side are probably water-filled holes created by blocks of ice separated from the glacier.

When you reach the ridge, follow it due south. You will feel as though you are walking on a bridge, and the view is captivating. In the valley on the left (east) is Stijguojávrrie lake, usually a haunt for a great number of waterfowl: it is worth scanning the lake through binoculars. Ahead you will also see the high, even north slope of Björkfjället, which swings attractively towards the east and forms one side of the U-shaped Delliälven valley. The vegetation is scrubby and difficult to walk through down there, but the valley gives inspiration to the landscape as a gateway to secretive lands further east. On the valley floor by Stijgguo, about a kilometre from the Trail, you will see a building and a bridge. The surrounding terrain is quite hilly with several moraine heaps.

After just over 2km, the path leaves the long moraine ridge, heads briefly down to a stream, then rather steeply up the side of Björkfjället to reach grass heaths, which are very easy to walk on. Continue up the fellside through scanty and low-growing vegetation to reach the Björkfjället plateau. The landscape here is reminiscent of a rolling prairie. In mist the plateau has a really ominous atmosphere, but in sunshine it is easy-going and gives a feeling of intoxicating freedom. In good weather, the plateau is good place to camp if you wish to break the stage to Rävfjallet.

Around the Trail you can sometimes see small mounds of earth, metre-high mounds with a tuft of lush grass on the top, which are used as lookouts and breeding places by Long-tailed Skuas. When lemming numbers are high they are probably also used by Snowy Owls. Björkfjället is a habitat for Arctic Fox, several fox burrows being visible close by. The Trail crosses the county boundary between Norrbotten and Västerbotten, which is also a boundary of the Vindelfjällen Nature Reserve, which therefore lies entirely within Västerbotten. Just before you cross the boundary on the crest on Björkfjället, the view behind, northwards, is magnificent, with the mosaic landscape around Sjnulttjie far away. Over the plateau crest new, extensive views await. The view expands as you walk along a raised area by Lisvuojávrrie lake, which is situated in a basin below Nuortta Lisvuotjåhkka (1058m). The peak's eastern side is a smooth, attractive slope hugging the water. At the north end of the lake there is an old Lappish grave, an earth mound covered with flat stones.

Just south of Lisvuojávrrie you will reach a fork in the path. Here, the old route of *Kungsleden* continued due south towards Ammarnäs. The new route turns off west, crossing a bridge over the Lisvuojuhke, then staying high on the hillside below Årjiele Lisvultjåhkka (1055m) to avoid the wet ground below. As you walk, there is a staggering view of the Vindelfjäll Reserve and Ammarfjället, across the Vindelä valley. To the north-west you can see Skebleskalet, a deep crevice through the fell massif, while to the south the steep summit of Stuvbiebákttie (1251m) stands out, forming a corner turret of the massif towards the south-east. Further south anonymous low fells spread out, allowing a distant view of Norra Storfjället (1767m) 50km away. It is a truly inspiring view.

The Trail now bends gradually westward and descends through wetland to reach the bridges that cross the Guolet stream. In its upper part, the stream has two channels, which flow through a split crevice at the treeline. If you have time, the crevice is worth a closer look. It is 30–40m deep and has a rocky promontory between the two stream branches. The east crevice makes a narrow cut through the bedrock, a waterfall cascading down into a small bowl with a pool of water where the ravines meet. A few hundred metres further down in the forest there is another beautiful waterfall, where water bounces over steep slabs, a cascade of whitewater.

Beyond the Guolet bridges the Trail goes diagonally down the steep eastern side of Vindelådalen. Between the trees you can see the long fell ridge of Stuorajåbba (931m) across the valley. The treeline is reached at the 760m contour, the forest being lush, with birch and numerous tall plants. The Trail fall steeply through the trees to link up with an old path through the valley, which is now used by four-wheelers and has become almost a proper road. Head north-west to pass the Aitenjas shieling, then carry on through dense forest for a couple of kilometres to reach Rävfjallet, where there is an overnight hut.

Rävfjallet hut (482m)

The hut is pleasantly embedded in dense and well-shrubbed birch forest about 50m from a ravine of the Vindelälven river. The noise from the rapids can be heard inside the hut, and through the north-facing windows the river can be seen beyond the trees. To get the best impression of the surrounding landscape, walk to the bridge. The river cascades through the 3m-high Rävfjallet, which is named for a Sámi man, Räv-Erik, who built the settlement at Aitenjas. At the ravine, the river squeezes through a narrow 'waist', no more than 3m wide, of projecting rocks. The 9m-high suspension bridge is downstream of the fall. Looking south from the bridge there is a fine view through the wide valley and to the surrounding hills. Northwards, beyond the fall, there are forest-covered slopes, but no fell summits can be seen. The hut has three locked rooms with altogether 16 beds, and a permanently open kitchen with two beds. The key for the bedrooms can be hired at the Ammarnäs Visitor Centre, at Bäverholmen and from the shop in Adolfsström.

Day excursions

1. The lush forest at Altenjas is rewarding for both botanic and ornithological excursions. Above the shieling there is a high precipice, another 'southern plant mountain' on which temperate plants are found, such as Redcurrant (*Ribes rubrum*), Raspberry (*Rubus idaeus*), Mezereon (*Daphne mezereum*), Baneberry (*Actaea spicata*) and Bulbous Corydalis (*Corydalis cava*). The birdlife is also abundant, with passerines such as Dunnock, Garden Warbler, Ring Ouzel, Blackbird, Spotted Flycatcher and Three-toed Woodpecker usually breeding in the area.

2. Another fine excursion is to climb Ájtelsnástjåhkka (1048m), an interesting viewpoint. From the hut, take the forest road north towards

Vitnjul, then follow the stream descending from Ájtelsnástjåhkka. The climb is steep, through scrubby birch forest. The summit is a ridge rising above a plateau that is circled by a system of moraine ridges on the 900m contour: the ridges are most prominent on the eastern side of the peak, where one dams a small, long and narrow, lake. From the summit there is an extensive view across rolling Björkfjället, with Riehkiere (1382m) prominent. The view across Vindelådalen towards Ammarfjället is equally magnificent.

Distance: about 4km. Height gain/loss: ±570m. Time: 3–4 hours.

22. Rävfjallet – Ammarnäs

Distance: about 21km. Height gain/loss: +540m, -580m. Time: 8–10 hours. Strenuous.

From the Vindelälven valley the Royal Trail climbs to a long fell ridge that is followed due south for some distance, with extensive views on the left side (north-east), and the high Ammarfjället mountains to the right (west). The stage finishes with a steep descent to the village.

Cross the bridge over Vindelälven, then climb steeply through dry birch forest. Initially the Trail follows the small Vuot brook to reach a small plateau on the hillside. The Trail is actually not taking the most direct line towards Ammarnäs, but is choosing drier ground on the high fell ridge, starting out due west, but then making a long bend to finish up heading south, climbing throughout. As the Trail skirts the edge of a large bog where the forest thins, the view expands. On the far side of the Vindelå valley you can see the precipice at Aitenjas, which appears to have been carved out of the hillside. Ájtelsnástjåhkka (1048m) forms a continuous ridge above the precipice. Ahead, as you climb towards the wide ridge of Stuorajåbba (931m), is Stålluoålggie (1155m). The view to the upper Vindelå valley is obstructed by the forest-covered Vuoddasássie (796m: the name actually means 'forest-

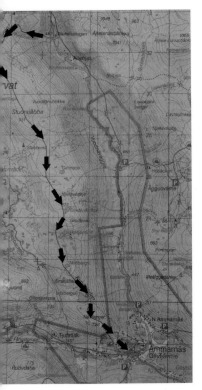

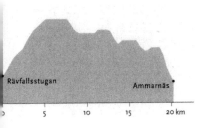

covered ridge'). Beyond the treeline, the northern Vindelå valley becomes obscured, the eye taken by the dominant peak of Riehkiere to the north-east, while to the south-east the valley opens up, Vindelälven glistening in the forest carpet.

The Trail swings round and up to the plateau-like ridge of Stuorajåbba. Beyond the summit, the majestic peaks of Ammarfjället come into view, with, in front of them, the wide Mársevággie valley. Rierruogájsie (1611m), the highest summit of Ammarfjället, is visible. The Trail descends diagonally towards the birch forest in the valley, the view ahead now dominated by the steep rockface of Stuvbiebákttie (1251m). From here, to the right (north-west) you can see through the deep cleft in the Skebleskalet massif: there is a path heading that way, towards Råksjávrátje lake.

Not long after crossing Stuorajåbba's high point a path goes right (west) to Stabburet, where there is an old Sámi settlement built towards the end of the 19th century by Jon Anders Grahn. On the open ground by the edge of the forest there is an

159

old dwelling house, with a stable at one end that can serve as a roof for walkers. The most eye-catching building is a restored 'stolpnjalla', an attractive larder construction on a thick pole, set against a background of a curtain of birches and, further away, a steep rockface. The larder was used as protection against bears, food being obtained by putting a wooden ladder against the pole.

At the path fork the Trail continues south along the oblong Stuorajåbba ridge. To the right (west) the mosaic-like vegetation patterns of the floor of the Mársevággie valley are rich in birdlife, so important that access is prohibited from 15 May until 1 August. Occasionally birds can be seen from the ridge: look out for waterfowl and waders, which frequent the wetlands and scrub in the valley. On the ridge, the bushy fell heath is also home to many species, while Hen Harrier, Golden Eagle and Short-eared Owl can be seen overhead. The views continue to excite. Beyond the corner of Stuvbiebákttie (1251m) lie extensive low fell areas, which reach as far as the high peaks of Norra Storfjället. Next to Stuvbiebákttie, the summit of Sulåjvvie (1352m) gradually comes into view.

You now cross Njallaváratje (840m) and Gieråjvve (840m), which form the long, narrow southern end of the plateau, then descend a short, but steep, hillside to reach birch forest again. Now continue on a narrow spit of land between the two small lakes of Tjaskáltjávrátje. The Trail then climbs slightly through dry birch forest. The view of the high fells above the tarns towards Stuvbiebákttie is very good here: as is so often the case, the peaks look more enticing when seen rising behind forest. Further on there is a small patch of open scrub heath, called Småfjällen, from where there is another fine view. To the south is Näsbergstjärnen ('northern tarn'). Behind this little lake, the depression by Gautsträsket can just be seen, but the Ammarnäs village is not yet within view. The Trail is passes another small lake, then reaches a fork where a path goes right (west) for Karsbäcken (the southern section of the Mársevággie valley). The Trail continues ahead, going downhill past Näsbergstjärnen and through the forest on the east side of Näsberget. As you descend the going becomes steeper. The

Trail now leaves the Vindelfjällen Nature Reserve, following a wide, well-trodden path to reach a ski lift by the slalom slopes on Näsberget. At the base of the lift there is a large car park: just beyond is Ammarnäs, where there are many possibilites for accommodation. The Trail is not marked through the village, so you will need to seek out the starting point for the next stage, on the far side of the Tjulån river.

AMMARNÄS –

Distance: 78km. Height gain/loss:

Between these two villages lies one of the most interesting sections of the Royal Trail. After each day walk there are fell huts of good standard, and the landscape is among the most magnificent you will experience along the whole route. The Trail starts by heading back into the huge Vindelfjällen Nature Reserve, which has most of natural scenery types to be found in the Swedish fells, the landscape varying from large forests and bogs to rolling fell plateaux, and culminating in alpine summits with small glaciers.

The Royal Trail starts with a steep climb through the forest as the walker heads towards the Aigert hut. The stage is short and offers glorious views. The Trail continues by climbing to the highest point reached since the Tjäktja pass in the Kebnekaise massif. Not surprisingly the panorama from here is vast. Beyond the pass the Trail descends to, and crosses, a

– HEMAVAN

+1640m, -1290m. Time: about 6 days.

plateau, before climbing again. This long stage finishes with a descent into a forested hollow and the Serve hut.

The next stage takes you across a hilly low fell plateau to Tärnasjön lake, where high peaks come into view across the water. From the Tärnasjö hut the Trail continues south to a remarkable lake archipelago at the southern end of Tärnasjön. Here, you cross bridges from islet to islet, a fascinating experience. On the far side of the archipelago there is a strenuous climb to the Syter hut, located on the treeline in the angle between Tärnasjön and steep Norra Storfjället. During the last two stages you walk through Syterskalet, the most dramatic and narrow valley on the Trail. In the western part of the valley is the Viterskal hut, from where you make your way down to Hemavan, where the 450km Royal Trail ends.

23. Ammarnäs – Aigertstugan

Distance: about 8km. Height gain/loss: +350m. Time: 3–4 hours. Normal.

The first stage in this final section of the Royal Trail is short, but involves a strenuous climb. An impressive canyon and a long stretch of marvellous views enhance the walk.

A few hundred metres south of the road bridge across the Tjulån there is a short gravel road, which leads to the large car park: the next stage of the Trail starts here. There is a Trail information board here, and a toilet. The walk starts along a road through coniferous forest: after about a kilometre the road becomes more usual forest path, and at the same time the terrain becomes undulating. Further on, the climb becomes more continuous, taking you up to a birch forest rich in plants, a sea of Globeflower (*Trollius europaeus*), Alpine Sow-thistle (*Cicerbita alpina*) and Wood Cranesbill (*Geranium sylvaticum*) covering the ground at midsummer. The Trail now follows a wide 'street' between the trees: if you pause and look behind you will see Ammarnäs. The noise of Slagerbäcken stream now increases: leave the street along a new route made for the Trail in 2005, taking it through lush forest to bridges over Slagerbäcken and Gåsbäcken. Continue through the forest, which is still rich in plants, to reach an imposing cleft, into which Ruovatjjuhka cascades. The river falls over 10m into this narrow, slippery rock crevice, which contains several 'giant's kettles', smooth hollows in the rock created by whirling pebbles caught in the stream. From the bridge it is a dizzying experience to look down on the waterfall and the kettles.

The Trail now rises diagonally through a veritable Garden of Eden, then levels out onto a wide mountain ledge, from where there is an unbeatable view towards Tjulträskdalen and Ammarfjället. Down in the valley, buildings and farms can be seen in the carpet of forest, while Karsbäcken shines like a silver thread in the dark forest on the other side

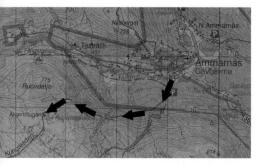

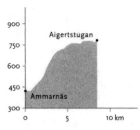

of the valley, mighty Ammarfjället rising above it. This view accompanies you on one of the most elegant stretches of the Trail. The kilometre-long and forested rock ledge which the path follows has a sharp edge on the right-hand side (northwards), the view over this having an airy feel without being threatening. There are some delectable viewpoints where it feels natural to stop and drink in the scenery.

Ahead now you will see birch-covered Ruovdatje (775m), which obscures the views westwards. Below the peak, by Ruovdatjjávrrie lake, is a marshland, which the Trail traverses to reach the strenuous climb to a high point from which the Aigert hut is visible. Here the older route of *Kungsleden* joins the current path. To reach the hut, the Trail sweeps beside the Y-shaped Ruovdatjjávrrie lake: for the last few metres the landscape is dominated by the wide slope of Äjvesåjvve (1250m).

Aigert hut (750m)

This large pair of huts stands on a small mountain ridge just to the west of Ruovdatjjávrrie lake. The huts have 30 beds and a sauna. Provisions can be bought here. There is good camping to the east of the lake. From the porch of the larger hut, the ground slopes down towards a large marsh, across which the Trail continues. Behind the building there are several small hills with scattered birches. These hills obstruct the view to the north, but you can easily walk to them if you wish to look north. To the east, parts of the rolling fell plateau of Björkfjället can be seen. In the same direction, narrow Rijbuovárdduo (875m) can also be seen: it lies just south of Ammarnäs and is topped by a radio mast. But the main attraction is is Stuor-Ájgart (1101m) to the west, with its steep and ragged eastern side.

Day excursions

1. The immediate vicinity of the hut offers an interesting walk for birdwatchers, the marsh being a good habitat for Snipe and Redshank. Recently, Lapwings have also started to breed here. Some ducks are regular residents in Ruovdatjjávrátje: look out for Common Scoter and Teal. Golden Plover, Blue-headed Wagtail and Lapland Bunting are often seen in the area.

2. Stuor-Áigart (1101m) is a splendid outlook summit. Follow *Kungsleden* a good kilometre south, then turn west to the northern flank of Uhtsa-Áigart (1076m). When you have skirted round this summit, a semicircular hollow appears: Stuor-Áigart has a smooth, grass-covered southern ridge, which contributes to the framing of the hollow. Cross the scrubby vegetation in the hollow diagonally and then climb, still going diagonally to the summit. The terrain on the climb is easy-going and almost boulder-free. A rocky ledge near the large summit cairn provides shelter against the west wind.

The view from the top is magnificent, with a dizzying steep slope down to the Tjulträsken valley to the north. This forest-clad valley is bordered by steep fells, which culminate in Stuor-Áigart. Across the valley there is a more gentle lower slope, beyond which the broad Ammarfjället appears. In the longitudinal axis of the valley towards the west, conical Tjuhkale (1420m) and Gábbie (1386m) come into view. To the south-west, the elongated Norra Storfjället massif is seen, the pyramid-shaped Norra Sytertoppen (1767m) its most distinctive feature. Lake Tärnasjön, the next objective on the Trail, lies hidden over there.

Down towards Lill-Tjulträsket you will see a delta, and by the Matsokudden several barns stand out in the forest. In this spot the reindeer herder Nils Sjulsson Rassa started a settlement in his old age in the autumn of 1909. Later, the farmstead was taken over by his son and daughter-in-law. Their daughter and her husband lived at the farmstead between 1941 and 1958, but since then it has stood empty. When active, the farmstead had five or six cows, a large number of sheep and goats, and a horse.

The upper part of Stuor-Áigart has an abrupt rock face, which plunges down towards Stor-Tjulträsket. The precipice forms a geological boundary, the whole depression around Ammarnäs belonging to the middle layer of the fell bedrock, while the high fells round about belong to the upper one. The boundary between the two strata also follows the steep south side of Ammarfjället. Stor-Aigert has some lime-rich mica schist, which promotes rich vegetation in places, with heaths of Mountain Avens (*Dryas octopetala*). In the scree below the north-eastern precipice you can find the delicate Small-flowered Woodrush (*Luzula parviflora*), a rare bicentric fell plant, which grows here at the southernmost point of its range.

Distance: about 16km. Height gain/loss: ±350m. Time: 5–7 hours.

3. Äjvesåvvjie (1250m) is also a good outlook summit. Follow *Kungsleden* southwards for 1km, then go straight up the northern slope, crossing meadow-like terrain. Snow remains for a long time on this north-facing slope, and the number of brooks on the map indicates that the ground is wet. But despite this, it is still an easy walk up to the summit plateau with its small, rounded hillocks. The view is not obscured by any high summits in the vicinity, and therefore enormous low fell areas spread out. The fells in the south and south-west are low and rounded, creating a soft landscape. Towards the north is the majestic Ammarfjället, while to the north-east is the plateau of Björkfjället. Ammarnäs and the ski slopes on Näsberget can also be seen.

Distance: about 10km. Height gain/loss: ±500m. Time: 4–6 hours.

24. Aigertstugan – Servestugan

Distance: about 19km. Height gain/loss: +350m, -280m, +140m, -260m. Time: 7–9 hours. Strenuous.

This stage is a long day walk at the highest altitude since Kebnekaise. You walk initially over rounded low fells, then down to a vast plateau and finally into birch forest.

The Trail continues due south from Aigertstugan, crossing a marshy area, then turning west, uphill, to the pass by Uhtsa-Áigart. In the lower part of the climb there is dense willow thicket, but this thins out as you climb. Below the highest point of the pass, there is often a patch of snow right through the summer. The last part of the climb is very steep so you are likely to pause: when you do, looking back you will see Aigertstugan with Ammarnäs in the background. When you have crossed the pass, there are no more buildings to be seen. To the north, Stuor-Áigart appears: from this angle it shows its beautiful, bowl-shaped bedrock strata. In the same direction, but further away, broad Ammarfjället comes into view, as does its highest summit, Rierruogáise (1611m), looking like a whale, and the black precipice of Suvlåjvvie (1352m). Ahead, to the west, a hilly fell plateau appears, with small, cone-shaped hills.

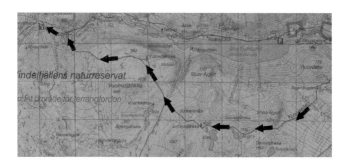

Immediately beyond the pass, there is a short section of walking on a slope exposed to the north, with great views, but then you descend into a shallow bowl behind Point 1112m, losing sight of the view north and Stuor-Áigart. However, you gain a view south-westwards: in the far distance, more than 40km away, the magnificent peak of Ryjvegaejsie (1413m) emerges. The Trail passes close to Tjålmure lake, by the shore of which is a reindeer herder's hut. The area around here is stony, with a large number of flat rocks, and the vegetation is dominated by dry and low scrub heaths, the landscape appearing barren and mysterious.

Continue along the south side of yet another mountain ridge to reach a new pass south of the small peak of Juovvatjåhkka (1099m), where there is a shelter with a latrine. This is the highest point on the Royal Trail south of the Tjäktja pass in the Kebnekaise massif. At the pass the panorama becomes amazingly wide, encompassing a large part of western Vindelfjällen. Below the pass, a rolling plateau spreads out towards the elongated and high façade of Norra Storfjället, which now shows itself for the first time on the walk from Ammarnäs. The peak will appear at regular intervals over the next few days. With the help of binoculars, you can see the flagpole at Syterstugan, 25km away.

The descent from the pass to the plateau is rather steep and arduous, and once you are down the high peaks appear as a distant mirage. Hardly any other view along the whole of the Royal Trail feeds the

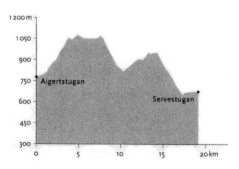

same illusion of a flat country like this one. In the west the terrain rolls on like a continuous surface, which baffles the eye. You do not see the depressions this side of the high fell barrier, so the plain appears to reach to the foot of the peaks in an endless expanse. But in fact, between that and the walker is the spacious basin of Tärnasjön.

The Trail crosses the path linking Dårraudden and Bielluojávrrie, then climbs the south-east side of rounded Vuomatjåhkka (1026m), a modest ascent, certainly nothing like as steep as the descent from the pass. The Trail circles Vuomatjåhkka, then heads down into a shallow depression between that peak and Point 982m where there is a shelter (actually set a few hundred metres North of the Trail). In the hollow, which is bordered to the west by a ridge with yet another pass that has to be crossed, you walk across a lovely meadow. At this next pass the view east (backwards) is interesting towards Stuor-Áigart. The fell projects like a plinth towards Tjulträskdalen, the north side being very steep, while the peak forms a long, level ridge towards the south.

From the pass you can also see the formidable Norra Storfjället to the south-west, but it is still a long way off. You can also count three small glaciers: Tärna glacier and Östra Syter glacier in Norra Storfjället, and also the mass of ice below Rierruogásie (1611m), the highest point on Ammarfjället. This summit has a distinctive profile, like a sand dune: descend from the pass with this wonderful view in front of your eyes. The descent is drawn out and rather steep and the birch forest has a great many insect-infested trees: around here the larvae of the Peppered Moth (*Biston betularis*) wreaked havoc in 1977–78. As the attack took place over two consecutive years, many trees were killed, leaving a park-like, open forest. Through the tree skeletons you can see small, steep Givjuovárdduo (880m), and the roughly shaped southern side of Suvlåjvvie (1352m), one of the most prominent landmarks in Vindelfjällen, looking rather like a tree-stump.

At the end of the long downward slope you reach the bridge across Servvejuhka from which you can see a striking, 15m-high waterfall, the bridge being suspended just above the top section of the fall. For the best view, take off your rucsac and and walk down to the basin below the fall: the stream cascades from a narrow rock cleft and spreads out into a triangle of falling water, an impressive sight. There is another equally impressive fall a hundred metres downstream.

Beyond the bridge, the Trail meets the path from Lill-Tjulträsket. This path offers a shorter alternative to the true route of the Trail from Ammarnäs. In the village, at the Ammarnäs Information Centre, it is possible to find out about boats that cross both both Tjulträsken lakes to reach Salvijukke from where the path can be followed to here, and on to Servestugan, reaching it in one day. From the fork, the Trail continues through the forest below Givjuovárdduo, Norra Sytertoppen appearing again. You walk past several marshy areas and suddenly find yourself by Servestugan.

Servestugan (700m)

The two huts stand by a marsh in the birch forest. Only a few trees grow here, so the location is relatively open, but the view is curtailed as the huts are in a valley. To the north the view is obstructed by nearby Servvetjåhkka (967m). In fact it is only to the east that there is any distant view, through Tjulträskdalen to where Stuor-Áigart shows its beautifully bedrock-lined profile beyond the steep rocks on Givjuovárdduo. The huts offer 30 beds altogether, and there is an emergency telephone. There is good camping by a brook a few hundred metres to the west, along *Kungsleden*. Alternatively you could camp by the bridge across Servvejuhka.

Day excursions

1. Nearby Givjuovárdduo (880m, 'the small mountain by the waterfall') is a rewarding climb. Follow the west flank from the hut up to the highest point for a fine view over Tjulträskdalen and the delta from just below the summit. The mountain has rich vegetation: apart from the commonest lime-loving plants, for example Mountain Avens, there is also Rock Sedge (*Carex rupestris*), Northern Milk-vetch (*Oxytropis lapponica*) and Small White Orchid *Leucorchis albida*). *Distance: about 4km. Height gain/loss: ±180m. Time: 2–3 hours.*

2. The large waterfall in Servvejuhka is also worth closer examination. Here you will normally find Dippers breeding, and in the pool below

the fall you can have a dip of your own, but with great care. It is a good idea to continue to the next fall, which is unique in that the cleft has a sharp angle. The vegetation between the falls is very rich. On the slope below Givjuovárdduo you may find Ring Ouzels. From the hut you can also walk upstream for a few hundred metres to reach some rocky steps with several small waterfalls.

25. Servestugan – Tärnasjöstugan

Distance: about 14km. Height gain/loss: ±120m, -230m. Time: 5–7 hours. Normal.

For a walk across low fell terrain, this stage is quite hilly, and also more varied than a glance at the map would have you believe. There are fine views towards Norra Storfjället.

Soon after leaving Servestugan you cross a small bridge, and then reach a steep ascent up over a rounded ridge. From the climb you can see, behind you, towards the east, beyond the roof of Servestugan, how Vuomajuhke flows in its cleft down to the valley. You will also see the precipice of Suvlåjvvie (1352m) above the forest carpet in the extension of the valley towards the east. On the high point of the climb the views expand in all directions. To the south you can see the relatively large Servvejávrrie lake ('elk lake') with its many islets, and, in the far distance, beyond the lake, Ryjvegaejsie (1413m). Norra Storfjället also comes into view, a now familiar sight to the south-west. Due west, the prominent summits of Tjuhkale (1420m) and Gábbie (1386m) can be seen, as well as the bulging low fells crossed by the Trail.

Beyond the pass there is a steep descent into a hollow and the next bridge. In the hollow there is scrubby brushwood vegetation with dwarf birch, and, usually, plenty of waders for birdwatchers to enjoy. The small pools often have Red-necked Phalarope, while Golden Plover, Ruff, Temminck's Stint and Redshank are also a regular sight.

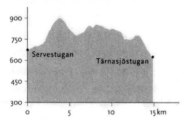

Beyond the bridge the path runs in a slippery, shallowly-chiselled valley between low fells. The terrain undulates, and has a pleasant, almost pastoral character. Several tarns give life to the country, ducks often being seen on them. In spite of the fell being low, the field of vision is, in part, restricted by the round hillocks. Sometimes you cross a slope diagonally, and when a modest crest is passed, the views extend in a new direction. The terrain is like this for approximately 5km, until you pass Siejdáge lake, where the vegetation starts to become scrubby, and you climb to reach a modest pass. From there you can see Norra Sytertoppen and Tjuhkale, both majestic, even if still at some distance. Peaks at great distance is something of a distinctive feature of Vindelfjällen, the landscape appearing to be enormously spacious, giving the walker the impression of walking in the middle of a vast wilderness.

From the pass the Trail descends steeply to the birch forest, passing Tjärven lake. In the forest there are some large, twisted birches, which restrict the view. Only small motley strips of bog allow you to catch an occasional glimpse of inspiring high peaks through a tracery of tree branches, but these glimpses allow you to appreciate the grandeur of the landscape. Now skirt a marsh and climb to the last pass. The stage finishes with a long downward slope to Tärnasjöstugan. During the final part of this descent, the forest contains plenty of tall plants: some private huts can be seen in the forest just before you arrive at Tärnasjöstugan.

Alternative path

It is possible to leave the Royal Trail at the northern tip of Servvejávrrie, walking south along an old Sámi path on the west side of the lake, later rejoining the Trail at the southern end of Tärnasjön. This shortcut means missing Tärnasjöstugan, but, instead, passing an old Sámi settlement at Tjielluo, which is well worth seeing. The settlement is located in a large grassy opening in the forest: there you will find a delapidated *kåta* and a well-preserved pole store, known as an *aihte*. The views towards Norra Storfjället are magnificent from the slope leading down to this settlement.

Distance: about 23km (between Serve and Syter). Height gain/loss: +200m, -300m, +100m. Time: 8–10 hours.

Tärnasjöstugan (610m)

At Tärnasjöstugan you are in the heart of Vindelfjällen, the site feeling remote from the rest of the world. The hut is well protected in the birch forest and is less than 100m from the lake. An older building, which belongs to the County Council, stands nearer to the shore. The view from the porch of the tourist hut is limited, but by the stony shore, where there are several sheds, glorious fell scenery opens up. The terrain nearest the water is low-lying, and the surface of the water spreads out hugely, despite your being unable to see anywhere near the whole of the 20km-long lake. Towards the west and north-west, however, there is a considerable expanse of water, the country in that direction appearing to have been hollowed out like a giant bowl. On the other side of the lake there is higher, forest-covered country, behind which is a long and continuous fell ridge that culminates, to the north-west, in the large double summit of Tjuhkale (1420m: the name means 'pointed'). To the south, the peaks on the other side of the lake are closer to the water, which narrows the field of vision. In that direction,

Rássjatjåhkka (1039m), with its wave-like profile, obscures Norra Storfjället.

Day excursions

1. The location of Tärnasjöstugan is an invitation to contemplation. You might as well spend a rest-day here, swimming or fishing. You can borrow a boat for excursions on the lake from the hut warden. A botanical walk to the slopes on the east side of the hut is rewarding. The local bedrock contains lime, and the marsh has many rare sedges such as Few-flowered Spike-rush (*Eleocharis quinqueflora*), Bristle Sedge (*Carex microglochin*), Lapland Sedge (*Carex lapponica*) and Scorched Alpine Sedge (*Carex atrofusca*). Along the shores of Tärnasjön there are also many different plants, including several high-alpine species. The water in Tärnasjön is exceptionally rich in nutrients for a mountain lake, and several rare waterplants grow in it. The fishing is very good, both Char and Trout being found here. The visible depth is, however, at most 'only' 10 metres.

Tärnasjön will also be interesting to birdwatchers, its surroundings being classed as a Wetland of International Importance according to the Convention on Wetlands. Several species of duck often swim in groups, especially Long-tailed Duck, Common Scoter and Scaup. Black-throated Divers are also common. If you walk south along *Kungsleden* to the marshes in Guhttávággie, you reach an extremely interesting ornithological area. Here a large number of species can be found, for example Curlew, Greenshank, Redshank, Wood Sandpiper, and also several birds of prey, such as Short-eared Owl and Hen Harrier. Celebrities occasionally spotted are Osprey, White-tailed Eagle and Golden Eagle. By the circular Guhttájávrrie lake you can also see Red-throated Diver, Black-throated Diver, and ducks such as Goldeneye, Teal, Wigeon, Mallard, Velvet Scoter and Common Scoter. The lake is never deeper than 1 metre, and has several islets. In the willow thickets around here, Sedge Warblers are often heard. The water vegetation in the lake is interesting. Among other plants you will find European Bur-reed (*Sparganium emersum*), Creeping Spearwort

(*Ranunculus reptans*), Awlwort (*Subularia aquatica*), and the very rare Shetland Pondweed (*Potamogeton rutilus*), which is otherwise found only sporadically in lowlands: its habitat here is unique.

Distance: about 24km. Height gain/loss: zero. Time: 8–10 hours.

2. The most interesting destination for a climb in the vicinity of the hut is the low peak of Deärnnávárrie (850m). The best route is to follow *Kungsleden* eastwards and to turn off towards the south after 3–4km. Deärnnávárrie is a flat and lonely little low peak with rather brushy scrub heath on its lower parts, but a plateau summit that is barer. The view is full of interest thanks to the peak's isolated position. Norra Sytertoppen (1767m), characterised by its commanding size and pyramidal shape, dominates the view. You can also see the whole of the Tärnasjö basin from the summit.

Distance: about 8km. Height gain/loss: ±240m. Time: 3–5 hours.

26. Tärnasjöstugan – Syterstugan

Distance: about 14km. Height gain/loss: +100m. Time: 5–6 hours. Normal.

This stage heads through the birch forest beside Tärnasjön to reach the remarkable archipelago at the southern end of the lake. Beyond all the bridges, there is a steep climb up the barrier of Norra Storfjället.

The Trail along Tärnasjön's eastern edge is essentially level, sometimes approaching the shore, sometimes further into the birch forest, a telephone line following and crossing the path as you head south. Where the path is close to the lake, the long gravel shore may entice you to enjoy a swim, or you can settle for the view across the water, seen beyond the rust-coloured stains on the shore-line boulders. Far away to the north-west stands Tjuhkale, a forsaken conical peak. On the far side of the lake you can see large, bright flat rock areas on

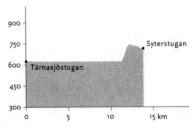

Juobmuobákttie (1139m). The flat rocks are granite, which glistens in the sun.

At one point the Trail moves away from the shore to an area with open strips of marsh and small moraine mounds topped by trees. The marshes have both scrubby and pure sedge bogs areas, and birds such as Meadow Pipit and Yellow Wagtail can often be seen. To the north-west is the concave hillside of Rássjatjåhkka (1039m), and above its crest the shiny flat rocks on Juobmuobákttie appear. The upper part of Norra Sytertoppen is also gradually becoming visible. After about 4km of this varied terrain, you reach the reindeer-fence boundary between the Ran Sámi village and Umbyn: soon after you arrive at the bridges that cross the bewildering archipelago of Tärnasjön.

The southern part of the lake is a mix of irregular shorelines, inlets and a conglomerate of islets, an area occasionally called Holmlandet. The islets are 5–15m-high rogen moraine ridges. Here the ridges are lower and not as boulder-rich as those at Lake Rogen (which, as noted above, give the form its name) and are characterised by a very sharp plant zone division. The northern and western sides are often blown bare during the winter and are therefore treeless, while on the leeward side plenty of snow collects, allowing both birches and knee-high scrub to thrive.

The Trail hops from islet to islet where the lake is narrowest using a series of five long, wooden suspension bridges. The sheets of water between the islets constantly change shape as you cross from islet to islet, and waterbirds can often be seen: look out for Red-throated Diver, Common Scoter, Velvet Scoter, Wigeon, Teal and Goosander. Common Sandpiper, Reed Bunting and Lapland Bunting are also common on the shore line.

When you reached the mainland on the other side of the archipelago, a steep slope leads up to Stokkeklippen, a mountain with little in the way of drama. At the treeline the views open up behind (east), stretching across the vast expanse of Vindelfjällen, a country you have become familiar with over the last few days. There is also a fine view of the Tärnasjö archipelago, its remarkable labyrinth of islets standing out, while the birch forest around the lake is as dense as a long-pile rug, the strips of marshland standing out. Further away, about 20km, enormous Ammarfjället looks like China's Great Wall, complete with occasional watchtowers. You will make out Rierruogásie, which even from here looks like a sand dune. Further east, precipitous Suvlåjvve still looks like a tree stump. To the south-east the forest spreads out, and far away is the prominent fell barricade of Buorguoke (1070m). Southwards, the landscape is dominated by the now-familiar peak of Ryjvegaejsie (1413m).

The Trail continues through brushy scrub heath past Stokkeklippen, then makes a short descent to Syterstugan.

Syterstugan (700m)

In my opinion, Syterstugan is one of the best located huts in Sweden's fells. The surrounding landscape is extremely varied, lowland and high fells meeting. To the west, only 5km away, Norra Storfjället has become a resolute bastion, Norra Sytertoppen (1767m) facing you, showing off its bold eastern side. In a semicircle to the south and east, the vast lowland provides an effective contrast, though there is a solitary mountain, Bånguoåjvvie (1059m). Further away a curtain of low fell ridges can be seen. To the north, the view is obstructed by nearby, symmetric Skijrátjåhkka (1110m), which hides Ammarfjället. More to the north-west, Svärfarsbäcken guides the eye to other enticing peaks in the northern part of Norra Storfjället. Nameless Point 1418m is a landmark here.

Around the huts clumps of birches mostly form low bushes across the undulating terrain. Further away, on the slope down towards Tärnasjön, the trees become taller and join together to form a forest, broken up by occasional marshy patches. Svärfarsbäcken flows below the ridge where the large hut stands, while on the other side there is a long slope up to Sjul-Olsaxeln, which hides Syterskalet.

The large hut has 20 beds, a communal dining-room and provisions for sale. It is locked during the low season. However, the older building is always open: it stands by itself on a hill and has eight beds. There is an emergency telephone. Camping is possible near the huts.

Day excursions

1. Syterstugan is an excellent base for exploration of the local high peaks. In particular, Norra Sytertoppen (1767m) is best climbed from here. The climb is a magnificent experience with some similarities to the West Trail on Kebnekaise, in that the path first leads over a lower satellite summit and then down to a pass before the final ascent begins.

The path to the peak leaves *Kungsleden* immediately after the bridge across Svärfarsbäcken. Climb diagonally up the hillside below the steep fell walls. The vegetation here is grass heath and meadow, with a large number of solifluction ridges. Ahead, Morhtejåhke (1586m, the name means 'bare mountain') forms a high and double-humped ridge, which ends abruptly with a deep notch next to Norra Sytertoppen. Below this pass the upper parts of the Östra Syter glacier appear, and above the ice Sytertoppen forms a regular and precipitous pyramid. The panorama is classic alpine. The streams on the hillside can unfortunately be difficult to ford after persistent rain: Mealhoejohke is the largest of these and flows in a hollow. Once over, the climb quickly becomes steeper and arrives at a grass-covered ledge, which would be a wonderful place to camp. The path skirts round Morhtetjåhke, continuing on the north side. The precipice is easy to negotiate: follow the red spots, which mark the path through the field of small boulders. The view includes the imposing hollow below Måskoesvaajja. The peak's name means 'the inward bend in a steep rock face with a protected grass plain', and is a good description of the landscape, as the hollow is framed by a semicircular hillside. Across the inward bend you can see a nameless lake at 1195m, exquisitely situated in a small hollow in the rock above the precipice.

The path becomes steeper and passes over the summit of Morhtetjåhke, then descends very steeply to the notch below Sytertoppen. The architecture of Norra Storfjället is strongly fragmented and captivating: on either side of the pass the two ice masses of Östra (east) and Norra (north) Syterglaciären can be seen. The ridge above the latter sometimes has a balcony-like snowdrift on it, and below the highest point on Morhtetjåhke there is a marked rock nose. The pass consists of flat schist slabs, which would also make a good campsite (at 1420m: there is a good water supply, the noise of trickling water can be heard everywhere). From the pass a boulder slope leads down to Norra Syterglaciären, which lies embedded in a narrow valley that disappears behind the precipices of Måskoestjåhke (1690m). In the other direction the pass borders the precipice down towards Östra Syterglaciären, offering an airy view.

The highly visible path continues a short distance from the pass out towards Norra Syterglaciären and then turns off up the steep shoulder to Sytertoppen. High up, large schist boulders stand upright. At the summit cairn there is a memorial plaque, while at the slightly higher summit (about 30m higher), to the south, there is a triangulation pillar. From here the contrasts in the fell landscape are overwhelming. This is the highest point in Vindelfjällen and also the highest in the county of Västerbotten. The view east is a dizzying leap into the air: the lowlands are spread out like a map, a terrific bird's eye view. Contrary to expectation, Tärnasjön is not visible, but down at the base of the east precipice there is a glittering, small, emerald-green meltwater lake in front of Östra Syterglaciären. It is situated in a perfectly symmetrical glacial niche and is one of the masterpieces of Vindelfjällen. To the west, the summits of Norra Storfjället group together into a convoluted and fragmented topography.

To the south, Sytertoppen has a tingling precipice along the super-narrow Syterskalet valley. On the other side of this abyss stands Södra Sytertoppen (1685m) with a long, seemingly unclimbable rock face, and behind this the massif extends like a high fortification against the lowlands, the summits lined up in a row. To the west, through the extension of Syterskalet, Tängvattnet lake comes into view, and, even further away, are the mountains of Norway. To the north-west, in the inner parts of Norra Storfjället, Skraahpetjåhke (1589m) reveals its sheer, bold precipices. On the whole, Norra Storfjället comprises rather round ridges and summits, the steep sides of the peaks giving the massif its bold character.

From Norra Sytertoppen a wide boulder-strewn ridge extends towards the west. About 100m or so down this ridge there is a bothy, a good shelter in bad weather. From the bothy you can continue on a path down to Viterskalsstugan. Leg-strong walkers might even choose to walk across Sytertoppen as an alternative to the *Kungsleden* stage between Systerstugan and Viterskalsstugan. If you are tempted to do this, remember that you will have to carry everything up here.

The usual return route is a reverse of the outward route. However, experienced rock climbers may go down the east ridge to the hollow by Östra Syterglaciären. This route can also be used on the way up, but it does require some climbing. The rock face is split by ledges in its upper section, the steps between being short, but steep and exposed, faces.

Distance: about 16km. Height gain/loss: ±1220m. Time: 6–8 hours.

2. A less strenuous, but nevertheless equally magnificent alpine experience, is provided by a walk to the front of Östra Syterglaciären, which can be reached along a cairned trail. Start by following the path towards Sytertoppen, then turn to climb directly up the slope to arrive on easy ground in the large bowl of the glacier. Higher up the ground

is covered with moss and bare earth. Once you have arrived at the glacier I promise you will be struck dumb by its high alpine character. The topography is absolutely in the same class as anything Sarek and Kebnekaise have to offer. The mass of ice, which is slowly receding due to the ever warming climate, lies beautifully set in the deep rock bowl, the cliffs above being high and steep. A prominent crevasse (in Swedish a *jökelsläppa*, a glacier fissure, more usually called a *bergschrund*) can be seen where the glacier meets the mountain. The strongest visual impression is made by the ice edge, which is 2–3m high and calves mini-icebergs into a beautiful glacial lake. The green water is dammed up by terminal moraine, nature's own regulation dam. Below the dam's gravel ridge there are small tarns set on a series of steps. The cliffs below Sytertoppen and Morhtetjåkhe are oppressively close, but in the opposite direction there are no obstacles to hide a boundless view. For plant lovers, Hairy Saxifrage (*Saxifraga cespitosa*) grows in abundance on the moraine ridge.

Distance: about 12km. Height gain/loss: ±600m. Time: 4–6 hours.

3. Skijrátjåhkka (1110m) (*skijrá* means the part of an animal's body which has been torn away by a predator) is a closer peak, just north of the hut, standing like a sugarloaf at the end of the long, but undramatic, ridge north of Syterstugan. The summit has a small cliff on its south-eastern side. To bypass this, take *Kungsleden* eastwards for a short distance, then head up the partly shrubby slope. The view from the summit of the Tärnasjö archipelago to the south-east from here is excellent. To the north you can see a small plateau, which leads to a marked hollow in which Rassjajavrrie lake lies, surrounded by grey mountainsides. You can continue the walk to this lake and then climb Muortuotjåhkka (1208 m) for a view of the fells further north. This is a superb viewpoint, as it lies between Norra Storfjället and Ammarfjället, a significant part of Vindelfjällen also being visible. The walk can now be continued around Rassjajavrrie to the enticing precipice of Rássjatjåhka (1039m), but you will have to wade

Rássjajuhka if you wish to complete the circle round Rassjajavrrie before returning to Skijrátjåhkka and Syterstugan.

Distance: about 18km. Height gain/loss: ±510m. Time: about 7–9 hours.

4. If you wish to do some birdwatching, I recommend a walk towards Tärnasjön. Follow *Kungsleden* down to the bridges at the southern end of the lake and carry on to Guhtájávrrie (or, alternatively cross the bridge over Svärfarsbäcken and follow the path south to get down to the many small tarns and the mire mosaic at Sleädtjie). During the walk you are likely to see a great number of waders, waterfowl and passerines.

27. Syterstugan – Viterskalsstugan

Distance: about 12km. Height gain/loss: +260m, -100m, +40m. Time: 4–6 hours. Normal.

On this stage, after a long climb over Sjul-Olsaxeln, you will be able to look straight into the perfectly symmetrical U-shaped valley of Syterskalet. The walk through the narrow valley is easy.

On the other side of the bridge across Svärfarsbäcken, a tough and in parts marshy climb to Sjul-Olsaxeln, a projecting plateau-like ridge from the foot of Sytertoppen, awaits. The ridge ends with a small knob, Vuekienaesie (1012m), where, in the past, reindeer herders used to offer sacrifices to their gods, seeking the protection of their animals against disease. The wet ground on the upper part of the slope is dominated by grass heath and meadow vegetation. The view to the east expands as you ascend, Ammarfjället becoming visible beyond Syterstugan, and the black precipice of Suvlåjvvie (1352m) appearing in the far distance like an old acquaintance. When you reach the top of the ridge and look in towards Syterskalet, a fascinating

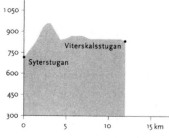

transformation takes place in the landscape. All at once you leave the huge expanse of Vindelfjällen behind and aim for the narrow valley in Syterskalet, a perfect U-shape between the peaks of Norra and Södra Sytertoppen (1767m and 1685m). From here the Norra (north) peak looks like an elegant pyramid, while the Södra (south) peak is more a cone-shaped colossus.

The Trail descends from the top of Sjul-Olsaxeln to reach Syterskalet, which has excellent grazing grounds so that there are often large reindeer herds near the path. Please do not disturb them! The Trail descends straight down hillside at first, then turns due west at a path fork, reaching a shelter hut with a latrine. (From the fork the other path leads southwards towards Solberget.) The shelter hut is on the local watershed, Västra Syterbäcken starting its journey westwards here. The hut is also at the start of the most dramatic alpine scenery on the Royal Trail: nowhere else does the Trail pass through such a narrow and deeply cut valley. Syterskalet forms an almost 10km-long corridor through Norra Storfjället, bending like a boomerang along its length, hemmed in by peaks that rise over 800m from the valley floor. The landscape feels claustrophobic, with only a hint of a free horizon, the rock faces guiding your eye towards it. The cliffs on Södra Sytertoppen follow the valley for quite a distance and are more consistently steep than those on the north side. The Trail stays close to the southern precipice, which has some avalanche boulder tongues below the rocks. The boulders fall down gullies in the cliff and gather in a plume shape on the valley floor. Some giant boulders lie close to the path.

But in spite of the black and threatening rockfaces, the valley has a lush appearance, its floor dominated by meadows and marshes. Tufted Hair-grass (*Deschampsia cespitosa*), Sweet Vernal Grass (*Anthoxanthum odoratum*) and Lapland Reedgrass (*Calamagrostis lapponica*) are common grasses in the green carpet. There is also a great deal of moss and bare earth. In the bogs around the river there are also patches of nutrient-demanding plants such as Net-leaved Willow (*Salix reticulata*) and Scorched Alpine Sedge (*Carex atrofusca*). Västra Syterbäcken meanders through these bogs, with curves and small pools.

Eventually, the northern rock face turns off further on towards the north, opening a view into Viterskalet, a blind valley hollow with steep rockfaces. You now pass a fork, where the path from Norra Sydtoppen joins *Kungsleden*. Here Västra Syterbäcken tapers off and flows into a small crevice. On the other side of the valley there are many small brooks on a large alluvial cone. These are formed by the stream from Viterskalet, which spreads out like a fan. It is now only another kilometre or so to Viterskalsstugan.

Viterskalsstugan (800m)

Viterskalsstugan is located where the valley bends and becomes wider, the site therefore being quite open. Towards the west there is an open view to the border fells of Norway, far away. South of the hut the slope rises to the upper part of Södra Sytertoppen, which is less threatening steep here. The north side of the valley is also lower and not quite as steep. Dålkoetjåhke (1522m) stands like a square block above the

185

smooth grass slope opposite the hut: a number of wet solifluction ridges are visible up there. To the right of this peak (north-east), you can see the rounded tops on Skraahpetjåhke (1589m). Further to the right, the great ridge between Måskoestjåhke (1690m) and Norra Sytertoppen appears. On the other side of Västra Syterbäcken, a snake-like esker can be seen. This was formed in a crack inside the ice, a sub-ice river then forming a tunnel.

The hut has 24 beds, a sauna, sale and an emergency telephone. Provisions can be bought.

Day excursions

1. Norra Sytertoppen (1767m) is a rewarding destination from this hut as well, using Viterskalsstugan as a base, also meaning that the ascent involves a couple of hundred metres less climbing and no necessity to go over intermediate summits. Follow *Kungsleden* eastwards for just over a kilometre, then wade across Västra Syterbäcken and follow the marked path up through the boulder precipices below Måskåstjåkke. The view into Syterskalet from here is excellent, the valley being really narrow. To complete the climb, follow the top ridge past the shelter to the summit cairn of Sytertoppen.
Distance: about 12km. Height gain/loss: ±970m. Time: 5–7 hours.

2. Daalåejvie (1337m, the name means 'the lonely head') is worth climbing, both for the view and the flora. To start, ford Syterbäcken just below the hut, where the water flows over a wide bed of stones. Once across, choose your own route up the slope towards Klovnjebaektie (1303m), passing a beautiful glacial niche with a small lake. To the west of the lake there is a projecting, relatively steep ridge, which you now follow up to reach a wide ridge, partly covered with vegetation, between the summit of Klovnjebaektie and the rising summit of Daalkåejvie. The climbing is easy to this pass, with few boulders. The bedrock is a lime-rich sandstone, which favours the vegetation and species such as Mountain Avens (*Dryas octopetala*), Bog

Sedge (*Carex limosa*), Northern Milk-vetch (*Oxytropis lapponica*), Slender Gentian (*Gentianella tenella*) and Alpine Fleabane (*Erigeron alpinus*).

The view from the top is extensive towards the west. Below Daalåejvie there is a small plateau with a sharp edge towards the Ume river valley. Far down there you can see the main E12 road (usually called the Blå Vägen, the Blue Road because it runs continuously beside the blue water of either lake or river) and some buildings. On the other side of the valley, Artfjället forms a hilly plateau, with the spiny ridge on the Norwegian high fell massif of Okstinderne as a background. There you can see several challenging summits. The highest is Oksskkolten (1915m), which looks like a chopped-off, flat-topped cone, but the most characteristic profile is the nameless cube-shaped summit (Point 1866m) south of Oksskolten, which has a larger summit plateau and looks like a medieval castle turret. Eastwards you can see right through Syterskalet: from here it is clear that the valley's northern face is less steep than the south.

Distance: about 12km. Height gain/loss: ±530m. Time: 4–6 hours.

Ambitious walkers can finish or start *Kungsleden* with this crossing of Daalåejvie. That will mean hauling your equipment to the summit and descending (or starting from) Klippen, a village a short distance north-west of Hemaven.

3. Viterskalsstugan is also a suitable base for climbing Södra Sytertoppen (1685m). The climb is demanding: start by heading diagonally up the steep hillside south of the hut towards a nameless stream that flows in a ravine. Higher up, there are often patches of snow, but the climbing is easier as there is a sloping plateau that you follow to the west summit at 1603m. From there you can walk along the edge of the steep precipice above Syterskalet, a 3km walk on bouldery ground with a view towards the northern part of Norra Storfjället. To the south, the view is into the Kobåsen ravine. At the

true summit there are five substantial cairns. The distant views from here are comparable to those from Norra Sytertoppen, the closer views including the hideous precipice to the east.

Distance: 12km. Height gain/loss: ±890m. Time: 6–8 hours.

4. Viterskalet valley is in many ways an interesting destination for a walk. Ford Västra Syterbäcken and then choose your own route up the slope, heading towards the stream from Måskoesjaevrie. The stream flows in a small ravine: Viterskalsstugan was originally located at the edge of the lower section of this. An enormous rockface encircles the west side of Viterskalet, beginning as a straight wall below Dålkoetjåhke (1522m), then continuing as two deeply concave glacial niches that are now icefree. Below parts of the rock face there are large scree slopes, while Måskoesjaevrie lake lies in front of the western glacial niche. In front of this lake there is a collection of high moraine ridges of great scientific interest. It is believed that these have been built up by a separated glacial ice mass, which remained for a long time in the niche as the ice sheet of the last Ice Age shrank. The separated ice mass then produced the terminal moraine ridges (which are up to 50m high), which are at right angles to the length of the valley.

In the eastern glacial niche there is another lake, though a smaller one. This niche is a typical example of the ice grinding the fell down. If you have the time, it is well worth going into the niche. Otherwise, continue into the valley that bends round the vertical rock face of Måskåstjåkke (1690m), Norra Syterglaciären becoming visible. The landscape now becomes very barren and sterile – genuinely high alpine, the valley feeling like a gateway to the end of the world. Continue across the boulder-covered terrain by the ice to reach the pass between Morhtetjåhke (1586m) and Norra Sytertoppen (1768m) and from there climb the latter peak. If you do this and then carry on down to Syterskalet along the path high up on the peak, you can complete a high alpine cicular walk that stands comparison with the best of walks in northern Lapland.

Distance: about 14km (to Norra Syterglaciären). Height gain/loss: ±440m. Time: 5–7 hours.

28. Viterskalsstugan – Hemavan

Distance: 11km. Height gain/loss: -40m, +120m, -260m.
Time: 4–5 hours. Easy.

This final stage leaves narrow Syterskalet, new views opening up west towards the Norwegian border peaks. The slope to the ski lifts above Hemavan offers fine views.

All that remains of the Royal Trail now is a short day walk. The Trail follows Västra Syterbäcken, descending easily with open views to the west through the valley. The 'valley feeling' that has been a feature of the previous kilometres of the stage slowly evaporates as the hillsides recede. After 3km you can choose to walk either on the old route of *Kungsleden* or the new one. The old one leads diagonally into a hollow and up over the ridge to Storkittleltjärnen, offering fine views westward, but is harder going than the new 'official' route, which

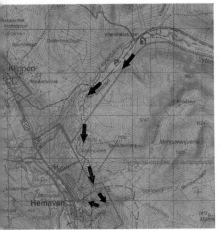

follows Syterbäcken to a bridge, where the trail to Klippen heads off. On the other side of the river there is an alternative to the Trail, taking a path straight down to the E12.

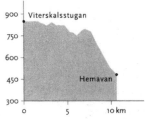

189

The Trail crosses the bridge and continues up the hillside, passing several tops where you can pause and admire the extensive view west to the Norwegian border fells, to arrive at the upper ski-lift stations of the Hemavan ski slopes. From here there are several routes down to the village: you can walk straight down to the ski slope to the E12 or you can follow a path that heads diagonally down towards the village. But the Royal Trail makes the least direct choice of route, staying more or less at the same contour height for a long time as it traverses undulating terrain with groves of fell birch: head south to reach birch forest. After a couple of kilometres the Trail leads down to the deep ravine in which Mårhtsoejohke flows, then turns back north to reach the Hemavan Visitor Centre, a building with a striking globe on top: from the globe there are good views towards the valley and Hemavan, and you can round off your trek with a good meal. Here ends or, if you so wish, starts the legendary *Kungsleden*.